physical education: an overview

BEVERLY L. SEIDEL, *Kent State University*
MATTHEW C. RESICK, *Kent State University*

ADDISON-WESLEY PUBLISHING COMPANY
Reading, Massachusetts
Menlo Park, California · London · Don Mills, Ontario

This book is in the

ADDISON-WESLEY SERIES IN PHYSICAL EDUCATION

*To Ike
and
To Our Families*

preface

The purposes of this book are: to aid intelligent, well-informed students, characteristic of today's college freshmen, to gain an insight into the broad discipline of physical education; to acquaint students, generally, with the organized body of knowledge embraced within the discipline of physical education; and to show the proper relationship of physical education to the fields of health education and recreation.

From years of experience in teaching an introductory course in physical education, the authors are convinced that the textbook for such a course should be characterized by brevity, reference to current research studies, and appeal to the inquiring nature of man. We hope this book meets all these criteria. All areas of the field of physical education typically examined in a beginning course are briefly covered; numerous examples of current research are cited; and questions are purposefully left unanswered so that students, given teacher encouragement and guidance, will be motivated by curiosity to undertake further individual and/or group study.

The prospective major student of physical education, for whom this book is written, is often confused by the interrelationships among the fields of physical education, health education, and recreation. Added to this confusion is the vexing problem of placing athletics in its proper perspective. Such perplexity may be nurtured by the limitations of the student's own experience and by the interpretation of these fields by the lay public. A perusal of the materials in this book should aid in ameliorating the dilemma.

All professions change and presumably progress. Chapter 1 deals with this topic and attempts to define the place of a profession within a discipline. The historical background of physical education, examined briefly in Chapter 2, helps to explain some of the problems and practices which characterize the field presently. Chapters 3, 4, and 5 introduce the student to curricular concepts and problems, including the now popular program of movement education. Current trends in education, along with their applicability to physical education, are examined in Chapter 6.

Chapters 7, 8, and 9 combine scientific information with a readable and practical application of the materials. Natural groupings, such as behavioral sciences and biomechanics, are used to present the principles and foundations of physical education as a discipline.

The history and current status of the interrelated fields of athletics, health education, and recreation are discussed in Chapters 10, 11, and 12, and areas of possible concern to the physical educator are delineated.

Chapter 13 deals with the professional growth of the student and with an examination of professional bench marks.

Finally, it is the hope of the authors that the professional appetites of the students will be whetted to the degree that they seek additional, in-depth knowledge in any one or a number of the areas of specialization covered in this text, since neither this book nor any other introductory book can do justice to them.

ACKNOWLEDGMENTS

The authors wish to express appreciation to the following colleagues for reviewing the manuscript in their respective speciality areas: Ronald Bos, Lawrence Golding, Jack Haskin, Heidie Mitchell, Paul Ribisl, and Glyn Roberts.

Further appreciation is extended those individuals and companies who granted permission to use their materials in this text.

Finally, we extend our appreciation to the anonymous reviewers, selected by our publisher, for their constructive criticism. Although all suggestions could not be followed, all were sincerely accepted and appreciated.

Kent, Ohio   B. L. S.
January 1972   M. C. R.

contents

Movement, a universal language. Photo courtesy of Lorie Coll and Ravenna (Ohio) City School System.

physical education, a discipline

chapter 1

A man who lives from a why *can handle any* how,
*but he who knows how, but not why, cannot
even live as a man.*

NIETZSCHE

Physical education has been an enigma for many years and to many people. At present the man on the street variously conceives of physical education as a muscle-building cult, as interscholastic athletics, as a play period. To some educators, physical education is a nonintellectual class, unworthy of academic credit, in "gym." The freshman physical education major, cherishing pleasant memories of classes and sports competition conducted in an informal atmosphere under vibrant and youthful leadership, often looks forward to four years of preparation in "fun and games" in order that he may spend the rest of his life reliving those memories.

> There seems to be a very general misapprehension, even among intelligent men, as to the nature of the work in which we are engaged. By many it is regarded simply as a specialty of medicine; others think it merely a department in athletics; others still, with more gross ideas, regard us as men who devote our time and energy to the building up of muscular tissue.[1]

Although the statement above, nearly a century old, seems to verify the accuracy of the first sentence in this chapter, it may also be interpreted to mean that the confusion regarding the nature of the field is confined to those outside the field. However, even professional physical educators do not uniformly agree on a definition of physical education, much less on the objectives of the field or on its place in the total educational spectrum. Little wonder, then, that the perplexity exists.

But times are changing! There is strong evidence that the American Academy of Physical Education, among other groups and individuals, has given birth to a commitment toward formulating a theoretical framework of physical education that is not only empirically valid but also functional—a theoretical framework that, once formulated, not only will be acceptable to all those who labor as physical educators but will also, let us hope, guide them toward program excellence. The beginnings were painful, primarily because no one had ever before truly wrestled with the problem of delineating a body of knowledge in physical education, but the product is healthy and it is growing mightily, nurtured by dedicated scholar-teacher researchers as they scientifically explore the phenomena of man, movement, and meaning.

The purpose of this chapter, then, is to discuss physical education as a discipline in order that the prospective physical educator can gain some insight into the intricate, diverse, and yet unified body of knowledge currently entitled physical education.

---

1. Luther Gulick, "Physical Education: A New Profession," *Proceedings,* American Association for the Advancement of Physical Education, 1890, p. 59.

WHAT'S IN A NAME?

Terminology and semantics have played significant roles in the confusion noted in our field. The school program in what we now call *physical education* was probably first called *physical culture* in this country. That term undoubtedly referred to an emphasis on the development of the "body beautiful" through gymnastic exercises, conducted to music, which stressed rhythm and grace. Its use was questioned with the advent, in the early twentieth century, of the "new" system of physical education—a system which stressed the natural activities of games and dance rather than the more formal gymnastic exercises. Today, although the term "physical culture" is still used on occasion by the layman when discussing the field of physical education, it is largely identified with body-building cults.

Physical training was the next term adopted when there was a shift to organic fitness, as espoused by such early leaders in our field as Edward Hitchcock and Dudley Allen Sargent. Although that term also fell into disrepute, it has never ceased to be used by some agencies, notably the military. When used in this context, it continues to imply an almost exclusive emphasis on physical fitness for a specific purpose, such as military preparedness or a particular athletic event.

Early in the twentieth century there was a shift to educational objectives when such leaders as Luther Gulick, Thomas Wood, and Clark Hetherington popularized the phrase "education *through* the physical." In fact, it is interesting to note that the objectives for physical education as proposed by Hetherington at that time not only are acceptable today, but are, in fact, the objectives embraced by many current physical educators. Since these leaders were dedicated to making the field more educational, its name quite naturally emerged as *physical education.*

Uncertainty in meaning still characterizes many of the terms we use. Just what does *physical fitness* connote? What are the differences between *movement education* and *basic movement?* Why are boys' interscholastic athletic teams labeled *varsity,* whereas girls' interscholastic competition is often referred to as *extramural?*

Adding to the confusion is the fact that, in this jet age, travel between continents and international exchange programs are commonplace. Thus the difference in terms and their meaning in other areas of the world becomes a factor. Some foreign countries continue to call their programs physical culture or physical training. What is *football* in Great Britain is *soccer* in the United States. *Gymnastics* in some European countries is what we call *physical education* in this country, and their *athletics* is equivalent to our *track and field.*

Current scholars in physical education are questioning the appropriateness of the title of the field as they consider whether or not physical education is a discipline with an organized body of knowledge and as they espouse a need to consider the theoretical rather than concentrate almost exclusively on the practical. Some of the proposed designations are ergonomics, kinesiology, biokinetics, movement education, anthropokinesiology, and exercise physiology. Regardless of the rubric, however, there seems to be general consensus that the field is primarily concerned with human movement and all its ramifications— physical, psychological, sociological, and philosophic.

Just as the title of the field has changed from time to time, so has its definition. Such definitions have run the gamut from the nebulous "physical education is education through the physical" to quite precise delineations of objectives, programs, and other aspects. One of the most recent definitions, which seems to be gaining acceptance throughout the country and is the one advanced by the authors of this book, is *physical education is the art and science of human movement.* (This definition should not in any way be considered synonymous with the "movement movement." Movement education is but one part of the total physical education program, and its role is discussed in detail in Chapter 5.) In order to illuminate this definition more fully, we will now examine it briefly.

When the *art* of movement is considered, the aesthetic quality of any skilled, graceful movement is involved—whether it is the dancer executing leaps and turns, the football player blocking an opponent, or the youngster skipping rope. The *science* of movement is employed by the track coach when he explains to a discus thrower the role of the body's center of gravity in relation to force and body levers, by the research professor as he measures maximum oxygen uptake during strenuous exercise, or by the swimming teacher as he applies Newton's third law of motion to an analysis of the flutter kick.

WHAT IS A DISCIPLINE?

Is physical education a discipline?

Many scholars have been concerned with defining and characterizing an academic discipline. Just as such scholars as Philip Phenix, Joseph Schwab, Benjamin Bloom, and Jerome Bruner have wrestled with the task of generally delineating the necessary components of a discipline and its basic body of knowledge, so, too, such physical educators as Franklin Henry, John Nixon, Warren Fraleigh, G. Lawrence Rarick, Ruth Abernathy, Gerald Kenyon, and Aileene Lockhart have been concerned with a specific formulation of the discipline of physical education.

Beginning in 1964 with articles by Abernathy and Waltz,[2] Lockhart,[3] and Henry,[4] through an entire issue of *Quest*[5] devoted to the subject in 1967, to a most cogent treatise by Kenyon[6] in 1968, many thoughtful as well as thought-provoking commentaries have been written on the subject. There is, of course, no universal consensus on whether physical education is or is not a discipline and, if it is, what its peculiar foci are. No doubt these issues will continue to be debated by perceptive scholars of physical education, both students and faculty. In an attempt to answer this question, physical educators must be concerned with a definition of a discipline, together with applicable criteria.

In the meantime, no one can deny that we have a considerable body of knowledge that is important to our field. That knowledge consists of facts and principles from many cognate fields, such as physiology, anthropology, psychology, sociology, biology, history, and physics. This fact does not negate the idea that *physical education* has a body of knowledge, since a body of knowledge can be—and indeed usually is—interdisciplinary in nature. In physical education, however, much of the knowledge underlying the discipline has been unstructured, and there has been too little concern with transmitting such knowledge to prospective teachers, as well as to teachers in the field. We have been too concerned with teaching prospective teachers *what* they will teach on entering the field and *how* it should be taught. Actually, a discipline is little concerned with how the knowledge is used; nevertheless, if we organize our considerable knowledge and transmit it to prospective teachers more effectively, they in turn should be better prepared to teach the *why* of physical education and thus become educators instead of merely skilled practitioners.

According to Henry:

An academic discipline is an organized body of knowledge collectively embraced in a formal course of learning. The acquisition of such knowledge is assumed to be an adequate and worthy objective as such, without any

---

2. Ruth Abernathy and Maryann Waltz, "Toward A Discipline: First Steps First," *Quest,* Monograph 2 (April 1964), pp. 1-7.

3. Aileene Lockhart, "What's in a Name?" *Quest,* Monograph 2, (April 1964), pp. 9-13.

4. Franklin M. Henry, "Physical Education: An Academic Discipline," *JOHPER,* 37 (September 1964), pp. 32-33, 69.

5. *Quest,* Monograph 9 (December 1967).

6. Gerald S. Kenyon, "On the Conceptualization of Sub-Disciplines Within an Academic Discipline Dealing with Human Movement," *Proceedings,* National College Physical Education Association for Men (1968), pp. 34-45.

demonstration or requirement of practical application. The content is theoretical and scholarly as distinguished from technical and professional.[7]

A definition as such does not tell us whether physical education is a discipline. We can say, for example, that we have "theoretical, scholarly content" but do we use such knowledge? Accordingly, it is well to apply some criteria to ascertain how well we meet them. Nixon, after reviewing several authorities who wrote generally on the subject of identifying and describing the criteria that must be met before a field of study can rightfully call itself a discipline, summarized and categorized the various criteria around "seven distinguishable elements," as follows:

1. A discipline has an identifiable domain; it asks vital questions; it deals with immensely significant themes, a specifiable scope of inquiry, a central core of interest; it has a definite beginning point; and it has stated goals.

2. A discipline is characterized by a substantial history and a publicly recognized tradition exemplified by time-tested works.

3. A discipline is rooted in an appropriate structure; it has its unique conceptual structure, and it employs a syntactical structure; the structure organizes a body of imposed conceptions (basic concepts); and it consists of conceptual relationships as well as appropriate relations between fact.

4. A discipline possesses a unique integrity and arbitrary quality.

5. A discipline is recognized by the procedures and methods it employs; it utilizes intellectual and conceptual tools as well as technical and mechanical tools; it follows a relevant set of rules; it is recognized by its basic set of procedures, all of which lead to ways of learning and knowing in the domain of the discipline.

6. A discipline is recognized as a process as well as noted for its products (knowledge, principles, generalizations).

7. Finally, a discipline relies on accurate language, a participants' language, to provide precise, careful communication both within its ranks and to outsiders.[8]

The mere listing of such criteria does not answer the question of whether or not physical education can rightfully be called a discipline. The criteria must somehow be applied. Thoughtful faculty members can wrestle with such

---

7. Henry, *op. cit.*, p. 32.

8. John E. Nixon, "The Criteria of a Discipline," *Quest*, Monograph 9 (December 1967), p. 47.

application; but so, too, can thoughtful professional students in physical education—graduate or undergraduate, doctoral candidate or freshman.

DISCIPLINE OR PROFESSION?

A later chapter in this book concerns itself with the "profession" of physical education and with the "professional" people within the field. It is therefore appropriate at this point to state only that a discipline is not synonymous with a profession. Kenyon emphasizes that one of the objectives of a discipline is to understand some portion of reality, whereas one of the prime goals of a profession is to make needed alterations in reality in order to improve mankind.

> If a discipline has curiosity as its motivation, a profession has as its motive service, i.e., the welfare of humanity. It is simply a matter of "what is" vs. "what ought to be." It follows, therefore, that arguing that a given field can be simultaneously a profession and a discipline is little else save a logically invalid contradiction of terms. The only solution to this dilemma, as I see it, is to recognize that, while it is possible for the same phenomenon to serve as the focal point of both a profession and a discipline (subject matter for one, a medium for the other), it is there that the similarity ends. Thus, the expression "physical education" with its obvious professional connotations, is not a suitable label for both the profession *and* disciplinary aspects of human physical activity. However, because of its widespread currency, and despite the semantic difficulties long alluded to, the term might be retained, but in a restricted sense. Those who would use physical activity to change behavior—whether it be cognitive, affective or psychomotor—I would call *physical educators.* On the other hand, those whose objective it is to understand the phenomenon, I would consider members of a discipline, the name of which is still the topic of much debate.[9]

It is thus apparent, at least in the minds of many current leaders, that physical education as an academic discipline is based on an organized body of knowledge concerning human movement and that one must understand this body of knowledge before one can learn to transmit understanding to others via the profession of teaching. Fraleigh discusses this tenet succinctly.

> ... it is now appropriate to say that understanding the nature of the subject matter precedes in time the attempt to study educational process either in or through the subject matter. Thus, in teacher education conscious study to understand the phenomenon of vigorous human movement precedes in time conscious study to understand the process of education in and/or

9. Gerald S. Kenyon, "A Sociology of Sport: On Becoming a Sub-Discipline," in R. C. Brown and B. J. Cratty (eds.), *New Perspectives of Man in Action* (Englewood Cliffs, N.J.: Prentice-Hall, 1969), p. 165.

through vigorous human movement. The following premises tend to support this contention.

1. Depth of understanding of subject matter is a necessary prerequisite to intelligent attempts to transmit it to others.

2. Understanding the phenomenon of vigorous human movement is not exactly the same as understanding the process of teaching in and/or through vigorous human movement.

3. The perspective with which a learner and a teacher approach the study of subject matter has a great deal to do with what kind of understandings come out of that study.

4. Disciplined subject matter suggests by its nature appropriate methods of inquiry to investigate it. Methods of inquiry of a discipline must be carefully integrated with educational process in the form of instructional theory in order for effective learning to occur. Therefore, the presence of a disciplined subject matter is a prior necessity to study of integration of educational process with the subject matter.

Granted the validity of these assertions, the importance of formulating the subject matter of physical education into an academic discipline becomes apparent.[10]

The focus of this book is on the premise that there is a body of knowledge concerning human movement and that students who are just commencing their professional study in physical education need to be exposed to such knowledge as quickly as possible. Accordingly, an attempt is made to cite the latest research and to acquaint the student with the vast number of library resources available in the field. We hope that, by the end of the course, the student will be better prepared to make at least a tentative decision on which of the many avenues available to him in physical education he may wish to choose. Teacher? Researcher? Coach? Dancer? Curriculum expert? Administrator?

Regardless of the answers reached to the questions raised in this chapter, one cannot escape the truism that "actions speak louder than words." If physical education is an academic discipline, the implications for the field seem clear. As discussed above, we must do a better, more thorough job of teaching the body of knowledge basic to the discipline to those students who are pursuing physical education as a college major. Subsequently, we must also prepare college graduates to be more competent teachers—teachers who not only understand the *whys* of their profession but also know how to construct sound school programs

---

Dance, one form of human movement. Photo courtesy of Department of Physical Education for Women, Kent State University.

in physical education and how to organize efficiently so that the *hows* and *whats* are more adequately effectuated.

In the long run, the entire future of physical education rests on the shoulders of those whose vocation it is. They must be respected by their administrators, their colleagues, their students, and their public. Quality in every aspect of the discipline is the only answer to the ultimate attainment of prestige.

STUDENT PROJECTS

1. Obtain biographical information on the leaders in our field, past and present, who were named in this chapter. What names might be added to the list?
2. Apply Nixon's criteria regarding a discipline to physical education, decide how well physical education meets each one, and justify your decision.
3. What objectives for physical education did Clark Hetherington propose? Why are they still applicable today?
4. Are other countries in the world concerned about physical education becoming an academic discipline? Make a list of selected countries which are concerned and those which are not. Try to theorize why.
5. What basic library research tools are housed in your university library? Why might it be desirable to make a list of them, together with their call numbers and the specific purpose each serves?
6. Prepare oral and/or written reports on specific resources from the periodicals in the references at the end of the chapter.

GLOSSARY OF TERMS

Physical culture A theory of physical activity which has as its basis the promotion of body development.

Physical training Use of physical exercise for preparation to participate in a specific activity or sport.

Physical education The art and science of human movement.

Intramurals Recreational activities carried on within an institution (school).

Extramurals The extension of the intramural program to include other schools.

Discipline An area of study characterized by an organized body of knowledge.

Profession The practice of a discipline within a defined context, such as a code of ethics.

"Gym" A commonly heard label for the school program in physical education, whose use should be discouraged. It denotes only the place in which the program is conducted and does not properly refer to the program itself.

SELECTED REFERENCES

1. Abernathy, Ruth, and Maryann Waltz. "Toward a Discipline: First Steps First," *Quest,* Monograph 2 (April 1964), pp. 1-7.

2. Bloom, Benjamin S. (ed.). *Taxonomy of Educational Objectives.* New York: Longmans, Green, 1956.

3. Brackenbury, Robert L. "Physical Education, an Intellectual Emphasis?" *Quest,* Monograph 1 (December 1963), pp. 3-6.

4. Bruner, Jerome S. *Toward a Theory of Instruction.* Cambridge: Harvard University Press, 1966.

5. Elam, S. (ed.). *Education and the Structure of Knowledge.* Chicago: Rand McNally, 1964.

6. Flaten, Clarence. "Physical Education as Inquiry," *Conference Proceedings,* Midwest Association of Physical Education for College Women (October 1969), pp. 35-36.

7. Fraleigh, Warren P. "A Prologue to the Study of Theory Building in Physical Education," *Quest,* Monograph 12 (May 1969), pp. 26-33.

8. _____ . "Toward a Conceptual Model of the Academic Subject Matter of Physical Education as a Discipline," *Proceedings,* National College Physical Education Association for Men (1966), pp. 31-39.

9. Gulick, Luther. "Physical Education: A New Profession," *Proceedings,* American Association for the Advancement of Physical Education (1890), p. 59.

10. Henry, Franklin M. "Physical Education: An Academic Discipline," *Journal of Health, Physical Education and Recreation,* 37 (September 1964), pp. 32-33, 69.

11. Hill, J. M. (ed.). *The Body of Knowledge Unique to the Profession of Education.* Washington: Pi Lambda Theta, 1966.

12. Jewett, Ann. "Implications from Curriculum Theory for Physical Education," *American Academy of Physical Education Papers,* 2 (October 1968).

13. Kenyon, Gerald S. "A Sociology of Sport: On Becoming a Sub-Discipline," in R. C. Brown and B. J. Cratty (eds.), *New Perspectives of Man in Action.* Englewood Cliffs, N.J.: Prentice-Hall, 1969, pp. 163-180.

14. _____ . "On the Conceptualization of Sub-Disciplines Within an Academic Discipline Dealing with Human Movement," *Proceedings,* National College Physical Education Association for Men (1968), pp. 34-45.

15. Larson, Leonard A. "Professional Preparation for the Activity Sciences," *Journal of Sports Medicine,* 5 (March 1965), pp. 15-22.

16. Lockhart, Aileene. "What's in a Name?" *Quest,* Monograph 2 (April 1964), pp. 9-13.

17. MacKenzie, Marlin M. *Toward a New Curriculum in Physical Education,* New York: McGraw-Hill, 1969.

18. Metheny, Eleanor. "The 'Design' Conference," *Journal of Health, Physical Education and Recreation,* 37 (May 1966), p. 6.

19. Mosston, Muska. *Teaching Physical Education.* Columbus, Ohio: Charles E. Merrill, 1966.

20. Olsen, A. Morgan. "On the Elaboration of Physical Education Theory," *Proceedings,* International Seminar on Research in Physical Education in Universities and Colleges, Paris, 1966.

21. Paddick, Robert J. "The Nature and Place of a Field of Knowledge in Physical Education." Master's thesis, University of Alberta, 1967.

22. *Quest,* Monograph 9 (December 1967). Entire issue.

23. *Report of the National Conference on Interpretation of Physical Education.* Chicago: Athletic Institute, 1961.

24. Smith, Karl U. "Cybernetic Foundations of Physical Behavioral Science," *Quest,* Monograph 7 (May 1967), pp. 26-82.

25. Turner, Edward T. "Physical Education: A Paradoxical Phenomenon," *The Physical Educator,* 25 (December 1968), pp. 174-176.

our legacy
from the past

chapter 2

Those who cannot remember the past are condemned to repeat it.

SANTAYANA

INTRODUCTION

From past to present, physical education has been an index of society—neither better nor worse than other aspects of society. Physical education has been used to bring man together for noble purposes, to indicate the virility of a nation, and unfortunately, to get men ready to defend themselves and their countries and, in the last analysis, to destroy each other. Since physical education is adaptable, it has been used and misused by the leaders of the past. The recent invitation to the United States Table Tennis Team to visit Red China in April 1971 was hailed around the world as a fine diplomatic move and the first step in the renewal of direct relations between Red China and the United States. As expressed by one commentator, the "Great Wall of China now has a hole in it the size of a ping pong ball."

The philosophies, ethics, customs, and even the economic conditions of the people of the times have been reflected through the medium of physical education and sports. As an example of the reflection of economic conditions, some of the more popular sports during the Depression of the 1930's, such as volleyball, fishing, and softball (without gloves), were those in which the equipment, though expendable, was long-lasting. In periods of affluence, boating, golf, bowling, and drag racing are among the more popular activities.

A study of the history of physical education and sports also shows that a decline in sports participation is often an accompaniment of moral decay and a harbinger of the decline of a culture. For example, sports scandals are not a product of this age alone. "Spectatoritis"—the increased dependence of peoples on others' participating for them—became in itself a sign of what lay ahead. This was true in Egypt, in later Greek periods, in Rome—and it is true today.

In any culture, the type of physical education and sports is influenced by the climate and the geographic location, by the physical characteristics of the people, and by the dominant religion. Throughout history, religion has both encouraged and impeded the physical activity of people. A number of our physical education activities and sports had their origins in religious ceremonies.

Although it is impossible to treat more than sketchily the history of physical education in one unit of an introductory textbook, the authors wish to give the student some insight into his heritage. The programs in this country are eclectic in nature, and their roots lie in many foreign countries. Consequently, some of the problems we have are the result of adapting foreign systems of physical education to our own programs. It is the authors' hope that at a later stage of professional preparation students will study the history of physical education in greater detail in order better to understand present programs.

PRIMITIVE MAN

Although he was preceded by Solo Man, Rhodesian Man, and Neanderthal Man, Cro-Magnon Man is the source of most of the information we have of primitive man. He replaced the Neanderthal Man in Europe and seems to have colonized the world. He left the world his cave paintings, stone engravings, and carved figures. Much of his education was physical since he was both hunter and hunted. His education was geared strictly to survival as he learned to obtain food and water and to repel his enemies. His civilization was not inherited genetically. He had to learn it and pass it on to those that followed. At first he traveled to find new sources of food. He lived by hunting, fishing, and gathering plants. Later he domesticated animals to make his travel easier. As he learned to grow food, he traveled less and developed his family, clan, and society. The clay of the earth, hardened by fire, became the first all-weather playground for his children.

Except for those events necessary for survival, dance was probably the activity participated in by most adults. When and how man began to dance is a matter of conjecture. We know that in most cultures dance was performed mostly by the males, as it is in the primitive tribes still on earth today. Among the "dawn people" of the Kalapalo Indians, who live along the Amazon in Central Brazil, this tradition is still carried on, untouched by civilization. Man danced to placate the gods, to bring rain, to cure the sick, and to bury the dead. Man danced in "sympathetic magic"; that is, by pantomime he suggested a result he hoped would occur. If he needed meat, he pantomimed the hunt and the kill. If he needed rain, he pantomimed the flowing clouds and falling rain drops. Primitive man could not distinguish between magic and science. Primitive man laid the groundwork for what would be recorded as history later. His survival activities became recreational in nature for future cultures.

THE FAR EAST

Although some think of the Far East as having the most ancient civilizations, the recorded history of the area does not support this assumption. Future archaeological findings may reveal the facts. The Far East had practically no impact on our physical education programs in the past, but at the present some eastern combative activities are being added to the curriculum. Empty-hand combat was the principal contribution of the ancient Far East to the present.

India

There has been a paucity of physical education and sports activities among the people of India. The military motive was nonexistent since the oceans and the mountains protected the people from other warlike nations, except for a few short-lived intrusions (that of Alexander the Great, for example). The hot, humid climate was not conducive to vigorous activity. Furthermore, the basic religion, Hinduism, did not encourage such activities. Finally, problems of famine and sanitation prevented any large-scale participation since the ill and the starving were disinclined to participate.

The art of yoga may have been the one outstanding Indian contribution to physical activity—although it may be difficult to fit that practice into any definition of "activity." Onetime claims that badminton was an original activity of India are no longer accepted since there is ample evidence that it was brought to India by the British colonist. India has had some degree of success internationally in soccer and field hockey.

China

The climate of China, unlike that of India, was conducive to participation in physical activity. Although the entire area had natural boundaries, such as the mountains and the sea, the feudal wars of the pre-Christian period gave the ruling classes the motive for learning combative sports. The Great Wall, built during the Chin Dynasty, was intended to protect China from its land-based enemies to the west and north.

As early as 2600 B.C., there were evidences of a system of "medical gymnastics," the first adapted and corrective physical education programs in history. Kite-flying also had its origin in China and was an activity of both children and adults. It took the form of a combative sport when devices were added to cut the strings of other kite flyers. Head-butting satisfied the most bloodthirsty fan; two participants donned the skulls or horns of animals and then ran headlong into each other until one was unconscious.

The early Chinese also had boxing in many forms, but their greatest single contribution was the development of jiu-jitsu. Jiu-jitsu and other empty-handed methods of combat were practiced by Chinese monks to thwart bandits since the monks were forbidden to carry arms. Empty-handed methods of combat were exported to Japan, Korea, and other parts of the Far East, where they were refined to fit the needs and desires of the people. Judo and karate are examples of this development. Although forms of soccer were played in many cultures, the Chinese played a one-goal game of soccer with a ball made of eight conical pieces of leather.

Japan

Although the modern Japanese are among the most enthusiastic sports participants and spectators in the world, their contributions to physical education and sports in the past were meager. Much of their culture was influenced by the Chinese, and so were their physical activities. They perfected the arts of judo and karate and spread these activities to other countries. Since their civilization was characterized by the feudal system for a long period of time, only the ruling or warrior classes participated in physical education and sports. Among their martial arts were fencing, archery on horseback, and wrestling. The nobility also hunted with hawks.

THE MIDDLE EAST

The cradle of civilization, whose peoples included the Egyptians, Assyrians, Babylonians, Sumerians, and Hebrews, was also the cradle of physical education. In all of these cultures, the military motive was present and the spirit of the people was conducive to an active life. Much of the male adult's time was spent in military service, labor, or sports. In the early history of these cultures, women were relegated to a minor role. A notable exception was the early Egyptian woman, who enjoyed full freedom and status comparable to that of the Egyptian man.

Among the physical activities of the Egyptians were horsemanship, hunting, and swimming. The last was considered vital in that a swimming accident might dictate a watery grave rather than the tomb burial that was so important in their religion. In Egypt the nobleman rarely danced except for religious ceremonies. Dancing was performed either by his slaves or by professional dancers. Other sports were wrestling, bullfighting, acrobatics, and some ball games, including a version of keep-away with a ball. The person dropping the ball became the "donkey."

The Hebrew contribution was principally in the realm of health; the practice of handwashing and the dietary laws had both religious and health connotations. The activities mentioned previously also applied to the Jewish people. Swimming as an activity was referred to in the Bible by the prophet Isaiah: "And he shall stretch forth his hands under him, as he that swimmeth stretcheth forth his hands to swim . . ." (Isa. 23:11).

Persia

Persia deserves special consideration for several reasons, not the least of which is the fact that Persian culture served as the connection between Western culture and the Far East. The Persians were also the first people to offer an organized program of physical activities for a segment of their population. At age six, the boys were taken over by the state to be trained for the military. They were taught to shoot, to ride, and to speak the truth, and their activities included swimming, horseback riding, archery, throwing the javelin, and using the slingshot.

As in the other countries about them, the women were kept in seclusion. Persians did not dance themselves; their entertainment came from professional dancers.

One of the weaknesses of Persia as a culture was its lack of general education; the emphasis was on physical education only. This weakness constituted a reverse form of the practice of separating the training of the mind and body, a distinct dichotomy. Physical educationists today decry the dichotomy of mind and body and insist that education includes more than merely the mind. By the same token, the reversed emphasis on the body, as practiced in Persia, was not educationally sound.

GREEK PHYSICAL EDUCATION

No country before the time of ancient Greece ever held sports and physical activity in greater regard and no country since has matched the ancient Greeks in their enthusiasm. From the time of the Minoan period in Crete until the Roman conquest of Greece, physical activity held a prominent place. Cretan sports included boxing, wrestling, running, bullfighting, and acrobatic bull-leaping. Women were both spectators and participants, especially in the art of bull-leaping, in which participants vaulted or tumbled over a charging bull. Artifacts suggest the superiority of boxing styles of the Minoan period over those of later Greek periods.

During the Homeric period, all warriors were supposed to be athletes. Some of their contests, included in the funeral games in honor of Patroculus, are described in the *Iliad*. The events were the chariot race, boxing, and wrestling; such prizes as a woman's skilled handiwork, a mare in foal, and golden, two-handled urns were awarded. These and other events are described in the *Odyssey*.

The city-state system promoted the development of the athletic festival, which later developed into the Olympic or Pan-Hellenic games. Physical education and athletics held different status in the different city-states. The divergence may be noted in an examination of Sparta and Athens. In warlike Sparta a small group of citizens controlled the slaves who worked the fields and produced goods. Boys of seven were taken by the state and trained to rule through military might. Swimming, wrestling, running, and jumping were the stressed activities. Girls between seven and seventeen followed a similar regimen, because the Spartans considered vigorous activity as preparation for living. There was very little cultural or general education for the citizen of Sparta. Male citizens stayed in the military until retirement at about the age of fifty.

Athens is an example of the ideal city-state. There was a balance between military preparation and a preparation for the social, political, and religious life of the state. Children played at ball, swings, and hoops, as children do today. Young women remained in semiseclusion while preparing to take their places in the family structure. Young men were educated in both body and mind, studying such subjects as grammar, music, and gymnastics. The gymnasium (merely a playfield) and palaestra (wrestling areas) were in evidence everywhere. Even in the later periods, when sports were criticized by philosophers and writers, gymnastics (physical education) was still well received.

Pan-Hellenic games

The forerunner of our present Olympics began before the ninth century B.C. The most commonly accepted date for the first Olympic games is 776 B.C. They were conducted for the citizens of the city-states as individuals; team scores were not kept. Games at four principal locations and many lesser ones were scheduled around those held at Olympia near the plain of Elis. The games held at Delphi, Corinth, and Nemea were the most widely known.

The eligibility rules for these contests, some of which are similar to rules for athletic conferences today, included the following.

1. Participants had to be of pure Greek stock.
2. Participants might never have committed a crime.
3. Females were not allowed to participate or to watch.
4. Participants must have practiced a specified period of time (about nine months).
5. Once they had entered, participants were not allowed to withdraw.
6. There were only two classes of participation—men's and boy's—and there were no weight classifications.

The officials of the contests were elected by the citizens of the local community and wielded considerable power. During the training period, they could eliminate participants they found to be unfit or not sufficiently skilled for the games. There were no preliminary meets, but this procedure kept the participants to a workable number. Then, too, the winner was not always the one who ran the fastest or jumped the farthest. The judges voted for the winner on both his finish and his form. Finally, game officials were empowered to have participants physically beaten for false starts and illegal holds.

There were many things wrong with Greek games and athletics, and from them we should learn lessons that are applicable today. The Greeks had their own version of scandals and fixes. Judges accepted bribes to vote for athletes who were defeated, and participants bribed one another to perform poorly in events in order to permit others to win. (Nero was once awarded an olive crown even though he fell off his chariot.)

A change came to the games when the prizes took on monetary value and came to include even state subsidies for life. Professionalism developed because of both the increased value of the prizes and the increased length of training even for many "minor" games. Sports became a full-time occupation for the entire calendar year. Near the end of the Pan-Hellenic period, slaves were being trained to participate and represent the different city-states. The ordinary citizen became a spectator.

The various events were not greatly different from those of today. Boxing, wrestling, and track and field events were refined to the forms in which they were later adopted in subsequent cultures. The one exception was the sport of pankration, a combination of boxing, wrestling, and no-holds-barred brawling, in which only gouging and biting were illegal. Because the loser had to admit defeat, Spartans seldom took part in this event. A Spartan preferred death to admission of defeat.

ROMAN INFLUENCES

When Rome conquered Greece, it was itself conquered by the culture of Greece, including sports. Olympic-type games were carried on in most Roman provinces. At the same time that these sports were introduced to Rome, animal and blood sports were also introduced. The latter influenced the nature of other games, and brutality increased. Whereas boxers had formerly worn leather thongs, they now wore metal spikes that protruded in such a way as to cut up the opponent for the entertainment of the spectators. Chariot races were often won, not by the swiftest, but by the one who avoided the pitfalls of trickery.

Spectators increased in proportion to the brutality of the events. The participants were largely slaves, and the citizens sat as spectators in the large arenas. In the year 394 A.D., however, Emperor Theodosius, a Christian, abolished the Olympics, and shortly afterward the last gladiatorial contests were held.

The large stadium for spectator viewing was among the contributions of the Roman culture to present-day sports. Gladiators were trained, housed, and fed in camps similar to our professional preseason football camps. One of the training camps for Roman gladiators was located in the city of Pompeii.

DARK AGES AND THE RENAISSANCE

After the fall of Rome, sports and physical education were of little or no importance. The Christian church emphasized the importance of the soul and the unimportance of the mortal body. Asceticism was diametrically opposed to physical activity other than work. During the Dark Ages, Christ and his disciples, who actually led robust lives, were portrayed with emaciated bodies and haggard faces.

Only the nobles received a good physical education. A nobleman's son had a choice of going into the clergy or becoming a knight. If he chose the latter, he started his training as a page (aged 7-14) and during that time learned the amenities of the court (eating, serving, using proper manners, and playing a musical instrument). Becoming a squire at age 14, he helped a knight with his equipment and duties while at the same time learning to ride, swim, use the sword, scale walls, and wage war. At the age of 21, the knight accepted his responsibility for protecting the land and the people of the realm from enemies. His was a full physical education, which included long training periods for tournaments and jousts. Much of our tournament conduct has been inherited from this period.

The Renaissance brought forth not only a rebirth of learning but also a renewed interest in the physical activities which contributed to a healthy body. Vergerius, Montaigne, Rabelais, Milton, Locke, and a host of others expressed themselves in writing concerning the need for physical education as well as for the training of the intellect. Most of them advocated a return to the Greek ideal of a balance between these two aspects of man.

During the Reformation, some of the religious sects renounced any form of play or physical activity of a recreational nature. This development had an effect on physical education and sports in early America. The Puritans in America, by means of public censure of recreative activity and passage of "blue laws," did much to hamper the growth of physical education. However, one modern researcher, Ballou,[1] disagrees with many physical education historians on this point. He challenges as implausible and unfounded the claim that the influence of asceticism was the major factor in the suppression of physical education. He suggests that Christianity condemned not physical activity per se but rather the improper use of it.

GERMAN INFLUENCES

The most influential development in the German system of physical education was the *Turnverein* movement initiated by Frederick Jahn. Politically motivated, Jahn wanted to unite the small city-states of Germany into a powerful nation. A

---

1. Ralph B. Ballou, *An Analysis of the Writings of Selected Church Fathers to A.D. 394 to Reveal Attitudes Regarding Physical Activity,* unpublished Ph.D. dissertation, University of Oregon, 1965.

conventional teacher in the elementary schools, he taught physical education outside the schools in the late afternoons or on weekends. Later he met with the same boys in the summer periods and developed a system of leaders to assist him. Apparatus was constructed from tree trunks and other materials. The movement was questioned by government authorities since the unification it strove to accomplish threatened the rulers of the small city-states, and Jahn was arrested for his political activity. Released after two years, he was forbidden to live within ten miles of any city.

Adolph Spiess made many of Jahn's activities acceptable as part of the school program. In the meantime, many of Jahn's friends became political refugees in the United States and brought with them the Turnverein movement, which continued to affect programs in German ethnic neighborhoods of the Midwest even after its influence died in eastern colleges.

SWEDISH INFLUENCES

Per Henrick Ling, the founder of the Swedish system of physical education, was influenced by Franz Nachtegall of Denmark and Guts Muths of Germany. Ling's first interests were personal, because he sought benefits to an afflicted arm from fencing. His later program of strengthening exercises, free exercises, simple apparatus work, vaulting, and fencing was based on scientific principles of anatomy and physiology.

His successors, Branting and his own son, H. F. Ling, introduced gymnastics for girls and medical gymnastics. Equipment for these programs was devised to take care of large numbers of students at one time.

The Swedish system of physical education was introduced into the eastern United States, and at one time it constituted the official program in a number of eastern schools. Baron Nils Posse, who came to this country in 1885, was instrumental in having Mrs. Mary Hemenway, a Boston philanthropist, assemble the now famous Boston Conference of 1889 for the purpose of adopting Swedish gymnastics in the country's school systems. Historically, however, the greatest influence of the conference was the decision not to adopt any "system" of physical education. This conference is considered one of the milestones of American physical education.

BRITISH INFLUENCES

Except for a few periods in their history, the people of England have regularly favored sports and games over systems of formal physical education. Even when formal physical education was included in the school day, the after-school periods were devoted to games. Many of these games were developed in rural settings. The Englishman continued to play after his formal education was complete, and sports clubs arose to supply his need. This pattern is still characteristic of the English culture. The upper classes developed idealistic attitudes of amateurism, which stemmed from social behavior. The English concept of amateurism, promoted in most of England's colonial possessions, is the main source of inspiration for amateur codes in the United States. To this day, it has been difficult to resolve some of the current problems in the light of this definition of amateurism.

Many English games were brought to this country, and they form the nucleus of our present programs. However, some have been changed to such an extent that very little resemblance can now be noted. Examples are the evolution of football from soccer and rugby and that of baseball from cricket and rounders.

DOMESTIC INFLUENCES

Before the colonists came to the New World, the Indians, especially those of Central America, were developing civilizations as complex as those in Europe. In the ancient "Sun Kingdoms" of the Aztecs, Mayas, and Incas, there were dances and games that had been passed on for generations. One of those games had many of the elements of basketball. It was played all the way from Honduras to the region that is now our Southwest. The Aztec called it *tlachtli,* and in the Mayan culture it was *pok-a-tok.* The ball was made of light, lively, but solid rubber. The goal was a vertical hoop made of stone and attached to a wall from ten to thirty feet above the ground. The player, who was not allowed to use his hands, tried to put the ball through the hoop with hips, head, or elbows. The spectator arrangement for this games, resembling the basketball arena of today, included courtside seats that were tiered for better viewing. Some historians feel that this sport is clearly an ancestor of the game later "invented" by Naismith.

When Europeans began to arrive in the New World, the very nature of the hostile environment dictated the colonial attitude toward sports and physical education activities. The people had to be fit to provide the food for their existence and to protect themselves from their enemies. Game and fish were plentiful, and the presence of both fresh and salt water promoted the activities of boating and swimming.

Although the religion dominant in most of the colonies frowned on sports, the settlers swam, fished, and hunted for pleasure as they found more leisure time. The men were each expected to give one day a month to the militia. The mornings were devoted to military affairs, but the afternoons were given over to races, wrestling, shooting, and other activities, including some "blood sports." One such blood sport involved having chained wild beasts fight each other or having a pack of dogs attack them. Another was the cockfight—an activity that has survived to this day although it is illegal in most states. Most blood sports did not survive, partly because hunting animals in their natural environment was inherently more interesting.

The introduction of slavery brought to this country a race of black people whose background of rhythm and dance influenced the dances of that time and has never ceased doing so. Our traders also watched Indians at play and learned their dances and some of their sports. The principal contribution of the Indians was the sport of lacrosse, first observed among the Canadian Indians.

As different systems of physical education were being introduced from Europe (Germany and Sweden), young people of this country were enjoying football, baseball, rowing, and other sports outside the jurisdiction of their schools. These sports had great meaning to the populace of a free and democratic society, and by the turn of the twentieth century, games and sports activities were supplanting formal systems of physical education in the schools.

CONCLUSIONS

Since the United States became a melting pot for refugees from many parts of the world, physical education in this country is a blend of many forms of activity. With its roots in the past, it is nonetheless adaptable to changes in the nature of the culture. Wars, depressions, periods of inflation, and sedentary living have all contributed to the changing pattern of the programs. Conditions of the present will have an equally great impact on future programs.

It is imperative for the professional physical educator to identify those problems which have plagued the field since its inception in order that the mistakes of the past are not repeated. Some of our current problems have historical precedents. Among them are the trends toward (1) sedentary living by the affluent, (2) acting the role of spectator, either in person or via television, (3) removing the requirement of physical education from the schools, and (4) using sports and physical education as political or social weapons. These and other such problems have been dealt with in the past by other nations and cultures. Lessons already learned from these experiences need not be repeated again.

STUDENT PROJECTS

1. Select one of the cultures or time periods discussed in this chapter and report on its impact on present programs of physical education.
2. Examine the literature for information about the origins of 10 modern sports, and report your findings. Include any discrepancies that you find interesting.

GLOSSARY OF TERMS

Medical gymnastics Exercise for the prevention or correction of physical deviations.

Eclectic Selecting what appears best from various systems.

"Blood sports" Sports in which the participants (animals or men) fight until one has been physically beaten and is usually bleeding. Examples: bullfighting, cockfighting, bearbaiting, and boxing.

SELECTED REFERENCES

1. Ballou, Ralph. *An Analysis of the Writings of Selected Church Fathers to A.D. 394 to Reveal Attitudes Regarding Physical Activity.* Unpublished Ph.D. dissertation, University of Oregon, 1965.
2. Gardiner, E. Norman. *Athletics of the Ancient World,* rev. ed. London: Oxford University Press, 1967.
3. Gerber, Ellen W. *Innovators and Institutions in Physical Education.* Philadelphia: Lea and Febiger, 1971.
4. Harris, H. A. *Greek Athletes and Athletics.* London: Hutchison, 1964.
5. Latourette, Kenneth Scott. *A Short History of the Far East,* 4th ed. New York: Macmillan, 1964.
6. *Quest,* The National Association for Physical Education of College Women and the National College Physical Education Association for Men, Monograph 11 (December 1968).
7. Rice, Emmett A. *A Brief History of Physical Education,* rev. ed. New York: A. S. Barnes, 1929.
8. Strutt, Joseph. *The Sports and Pastimes of the People of England.* London: William Tegg, 1850.
9. Van Dalen, Deobald B., Elmer D. Mitchell, and Bruce L. Bennett. *A World History of Physical Education.* New York: Prentice-Hall, 1953.

10. Vendien, C. Lynn, and John E. Nixon. *The World Today in Health, Physical Education and Recreation.* Englewood Cliffs, N.J.: Prentice-Hall, 1968.

11. von Hagen, Victor Wolfgang. *The Ancient Sun Kingdoms of the Americas.* Cleveland: World, 1961.

curricular concepts

chapter 3

*Theorizing (about curriculum construction) is fun as
long as there are no standards involved. I predict that
it is going to be much less fun in the future.*

ROBERT M. W. TRAVERS

The term *curriculum* is variously defined and just as variously used (and misused). This fact may be of little consequence to the student beginning his professional study, but in order to motivate at least some initial concern about the program of studies being followed, this chapter deals primarily with curricular concepts, past and present. In it we attempt to delineate the place of curriculum theory within the discipline of physical education.

INTERRELATIONSHIPS OF AIMS, OBJECTIVES, AND CURRICULUM

A *curriculum* is a structured series of intended learning outcomes, with the learner as the focal point in both formal and informal situations. It is apparent that this definition, rather than restricting itself to the traditional concept of formalized classroom instruction, includes such programs as intramural activities. If one accepts this definition, attention must be centered on the results of instruction, and thus objectives in terms of behavioral outcomes must be defined. This approach is in almost direct opposition to the traditional one in physical education, or any other subject, which prescribes instructional content as a means of achieving certain generalized objectives revolving around the acquisition of skill, knowledge, and attitudes. For example, the objective "to inculcate desirable social attitudes," though laudable, is so nebulous that it is perhaps more often than not overlooked by the teacher as he plans for and organizes his instructional efforts. However, the objective "to assign to all squads the decision-making about the sharing of responsibility for setting up gymnastic equipment" is much more specific and much more easily evaluated, as well as designed to meet a "social" objective.

Regardless of the way objectives are stated, objectives per se are important if a true learning situation is to be structured. Inattention to the aims and purposes of education produces little more than a hodgepodge of "learning." Therefore, many educationists engage in philosophic discussions of what the aims of education in a particular society *ought* to be and of how best to proceed toward achieving them. The results of such study are manifested in curricular change.

The student who is preparing to become a teacher is exposed to the terms *aims* and *objectives* constantly. It is well, then, to formulate a working definition of them at the outset. An *aim* can be compared to the "impossible dream" of the Man of LaMancha or to Robert Browning's thought: "A man's reach should exceed his grasp, or what's a heaven for?" In other words, an aim is a statement of purpose so lofty as to be practically unattainable; whether it is reachable or not, however, there should be a ceaseless striving toward it. An *objective,* on the other hand, can be attained; it is but a rung on the ladder one climbs, a step at a time, in an all-out effort to achieve the purposes of education.

Any subject matter area in the total curriculum should contribute in some manner to the purposes of education. If it cannot, its place in the total educational perspective can properly be challenged. Therefore, the selection of curricular materials within a subject area is based, to a significant extent, on how well they can meet the objectives and aims of the subject and thus, ultimately, of education. This interrelationship is illustrated in Fig. 3.1. Note that no one phase can be an entity unto itself. Just as the content of the program contributes to the aims of education, so, too, the aims of education dictate curricular content.

Statements of aims and objectives for the discipline of physical education and for its component parts are abundant in the professional literature, and some examples can be found in Chapter 4. The major emphasis in this chapter is on curriculum per se. However, pioneer attempts at classifying educational goals should be mentioned, since references to these generally applauded efforts are numerous in the professional literature. The original researchers found that most objectives could be covered by three domains, or classifications: (1) the *cognitive* domain, which encompasses those objectives which deal with intellectual emphases; (2) the *affective* domain, which includes objectives addressed to attitudes, appreciations, values, interests, and feelings; and (3) the *psychomotor*

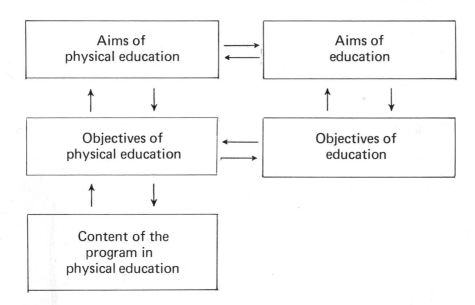

Figure 3.1

domain, which emphasizes motor skills and neuromuscular coordination.[1,2] The developed taxonomies (classifications) are of assistance to curriculum builders because they help to specify objectives "so that it becomes easier to plan learning experiences and prepare evaluative devices."[3]

Although the original researchers have not yet published a third volume in the series dealing with the psychomotor domain, Simpson[4] has tentatively classified this domain in a manner that should prove useful to physical educators. However, this area should give the physical educator the least concern, since he is typically more capable of specifying objectives in the psychomotor domain than in the cognitive and affective domains.

FACTORS INFLUENCING CURRICULAR CHANGE

The curriculum in physical education, as in any other subject, has undergone many and sometimes quite significant changes. Unlike the situation with some other subjects, however, the influences behind curricular revision in physical education have generally not come from within the school system itself or even from the state supervisors of physical education, whose chief function, at least theoretically, is the motivation of excellence. As an example, one need mention only the change in program content in physical education brought about by the Kraus-Weber report on the lack of physical fitness in American youth.

Although physical education was introduced into the school curriculum in the last part of the nineteenth century, until very recently there had been only one national-level effort, in 1929, aimed at developing guidelines for a comprehensive physical education curriculum. The guidelines published at that time were reexamined periodically, but no comprehensive attempt to evaluate them in light of contemporary educational philosophy under the aegis of national leadership was made until 1963, when a curriculum commission was established and funded by the American Association for Health, Physical Education and Recreation. This commission is charged with the task of examining curricula in physical education in light of current research in education, and to date (1972) it has reached agreement on the following points.

1. Current physical education curricula are a hodgepodge of activities with no pattern of consistency within them.

1. Benjamin S. Bloom (ed.), *Taxonomy of Educational Objectives, Handbook I: Cognitive Domain* (New York: David McKay, 1956).

2. David R. Kratwohl, Benjamin S. Bloom, and Bertram Masia, *Taxonomy of Educational Objectives. Handbook II: Affective Domain* (New York: David McKay, 1964).

3. Bloom, *op. cit.,* p. 2.

4. Elizabeth J. Simpson, *The Classification of Educational Objectives: Psychomotor Domain* (Urbana: University of Illinois Press, 1966).

2. The resultant learnings from these curricula, at best, are not relevant to personal needs.

3. To be meaningful, physical education curricula must be constructed within a comprehensive conceptual framework.

4. The development of such a framework requires the diligent, long-term effort of many physical educators with diverse areas of specialization and expertise.[5]

It seems safe to say that curricular changes in the past were based largely on practical problems, not theoretical concepts. Change so based can hardly be productive of the best learning. What are some of the factors, then, that ought to be considered if curricular change is to be more meaningful?

National influences run the gamut from professional guidance and direction given by national professional organizations to a determination of the social needs of American youth. Those needs must be examined by the professional before specific curricular avenues can be constructed. The federal government also constitutes a national influence through its subsidization of many school programs and its funding of research grants to study curricular problems.

Greater attention to *empirical evidence* of the needs of students at various developmental stages is another factor influencing change. Whereas untested and unproven "theories" were used in the past as springboards for program change, research in education is sufficiently sophisticated today so that educational theorists are basing their explanation of specific student needs and their proposals for meeting these needs on verifiable evidence.

The *knowledge explosion,* dating back to 1957 and the launching of Sputnik, was an influencing factor of great magnitude. At the time, the public panicked and there was widespread criticism of education by lay people. Educators tended to overreact by emphasizing acquisition of knowledge to the exclusion of almost all other educational objectives. Nevertheless, the fact that knowledge increased tremendously and that a body of knowledge was delineated in physical education laid the groundwork for dramatic curricular change.

The *change in value systems* from one era to another cannot help being influential in changing curricular concepts. Educators are wrestling with the philosophic question of what values *ought* to be stressed in American society. Differing philosophic viewpoints produce different value continua, but there needs to be at least basic agreement on a theoretical framework of values from which curriculum makers can construct models for action.

---

5. Anita Aldrich, *Cooperative Development of Design for Long-Term Research Project Directed Toward the Identification and Evaluation of a Conceptual Framework for the Curriculum in Physical Education, Grades K-16* (Washington: American Association for Health, Physical Education and Recreation, 1967), pp. 1-2.

A listing of the factors cited above, though by no means exhaustive, would be flexible enough to permit a more sophisticated delineation of factors which influence curricular change within its framework. For example, greater attention to empirical evidence can provide answers to questions revolving around such matters as personality needs of children and abilities of children to learn specific content at certain developmental stages.

IMPLICATIONS FOR PHYSICAL EDUCATION

Nearly all contemporary thinking about the process of curriculum development and change revolves around conceptual systems and theoretical models. According to Goodlad,[6] a *conceptual system* identifies: (1) major questions that need to be answered in curriculum development, (2) elements that bind those questions into some kind of system, (3) subordinate questions, and (4) sources of data that can be used to answer the initial questions. On the other hand, a *theoretical model* is "a visual, diagrammatic or three-dimensional representation of the interlocking elements of a conceptual system."[7]

Curriculum theorists in physical education are no exception to this "new breed" of educationists, and most of the recent literature in physical education curriculum construction also follows a "conceptual system" and "theoretical model" approach.

Perhaps the single most cogent treatment of the implications of curriculum theory for physical education is that by Jewett[8] in a recent issue of *The Academy Papers.* What follows is an attempt to summarize succinctly the five implications she discusses and analyzes.

1. The concept approach to curriculum development in physical education is most productive of significant improvement. Its potential, therefore, should be vigorously and scientifically pursued.

2. The problem of defining physical education and delineating its body of knowledge must be attacked with renewed vigor.

3. An acceptable conceptual (theoretical) model for the curriculum in physical education must be constructed. Existing models, both within and without the discipline of physical education, are not necessarily the most satisfactory ones.

---

6. John I. Goodlad, "Curriculum: The State of the Field," *Review of Educational Research,* **30** (June 1960), pp. 195-196.

7. Elizabeth C. Wilson, "A Model for Action," in *Rational Planning in Curriculum and Instruction* (Washington: National Education Association, 1967), p. 165.

8. Ann E. Jewett, "Implications from Curriculum Theory for Physical Education," *The Academy Papers,* **2** (October 1968), pp. 10-18.

4. Statements of objectives for physical education curricula must be drastically improved. Traditional statements are far too generalized; descriptions of specific behavioral outcomes are needed.

5. The problems of professional specialization within the discipline of physical education need to be analyzed more objectively. Therefore graduate study of curriculum must be encouraged as much as research in exercise physiology, sociology and psychology of sports, and other more commonly accepted areas.

SUMMARY

Attempts at curriculum renovation have blossomed in the past few years. Even though sometimes quite dramatic, much of this activity has been fragmented and nonproductive. For example, the introduction of television teaching is innovative but not necessarily indicative of genuine curricular improvement. Team teaching, though in general a commendable practice, does not guarantee efficient learning. Attention should be directed, then, toward a more global concept of curriculum in order to ensure true progress toward an effective educational system. However, direction signals cannot be more distinctly charted until the study of curriculum becomes one of recognized importance and until special curricular research competencies are developed and nurtured among physical education scholars. Genuine progress is being made; yet much remains to be done.

STUDENT PROJECTS

1. With the class divided into three sections, research and report on the three taxonomies of objectives listed. Select a specific activity and classify the objectives for it according to these taxonomies.

2. Review the theoretical models in some of the selected references (e.g., Galloway, Jewett, and Vogel). Are they similar conceptually? In what ways are they dissimilar?

3. Review the catalogs from some of the universities which have reputations for excellent programs in professional physical education. Are the requirements similar? Does there seem to be evidence of a conceptual approach to these curricula?

GLOSSARY OF TERMS

Curriculum   A structured series of intended learning outcomes. It can be formal or informal, in-class or extra-class.

Aim   A philosophic statement of an educational goal which is purposely remote.

Objective   A less remote statement of an educational goal. Objectives are usually characterized as "general" (broad in scope) or "specific" (limited in scope).

Taxonomy of objectives   A classification of objectives so that those similar in nature are grouped together under a common heading.

Cognitive domain   Those objectives which deal with intellectual emphases.

Affective domain   Those objectives which deal with attitudes, appreciations, feelings, and values.

Psychomotor domain   Those objectives which deal with motor skills and neuromuscular coordination.

Concept   A key idea which is complete and therefore meaningful to the learner.

Model   A visual representation of a concept.

SELECTED REFERENCES

1. Alley, Louis E. "Research and the Curriculum in Physical Education," in *Research Methods in Health, Physical Education and Recreation*, 2nd ed. Washington: American Association for Health, Physical Education and Recreation, 1959.

2. Bloom, Benjamin S. (ed.). *Taxonomy of Educational Objectives. Handbook I: Cognitive Domain*. New York: David McKay, 1956.

3. Brown, Camille, and Rosalind Cassidy. *Theory in Physical Education.* Philadelphia: Lea and Febiger, 1963.

4. Clein, Marvin, and William J. Stone. "Physical Education and the Classification of Educational Objectives: Psychomotor Domain." *Physical Educator,* 27 (March 1970), pp. 34-35.

5. Conner, Forrest E., and William J. Ellena (eds.). *Curriculum Handbook for School Administrators.* Washington: American Association of School Administrators, 1967.

6. Cowell, Charles C., and Helen Hazelton. *Curriculum Designs in Physical Education.* Englewood Cliffs, N.J.: Prentice-Hall, 1959.

7. Galloway, June P. *A Conceptual Approach for Determining Patterns of Professional Preparation for Women in Health and Physical Education.* Unpublished Ed.D. dissertation, University of North Carolina, Greensboro, 1969.

8. Goodlad, John I. "Curriculum: The State of the Field," *Review of Educational Research,* 30 (June 1960).

9. Jewett, Ann E. "Implications from Curriculum Theory for Physical Education," *The Academy Papers,* 2 (October 1968).

10. Kratwohl, David R., Benjamin S. Bloom, and Bertram Masia. *Taxonomy of Educational Objectives. Handbook II: Affective Domain.* New York: David McKay, 1964.

11. MacKenzie, Marlin M. *Toward a New Curriculum in Physical Education.* McGraw-Hill, 1969.

12. Marconnit, George D., and Edmund C. Short (eds.). *Contemporary Thought on Public School Curriculum.* Dubuque, Iowa: W. C. Brown, 1968.

13. National Education Association, Center for the Study of Instruction. "Curriculum for People," *Today's Education,* 60 (February 1971), pp. 42-44.

14. National Education Association, Center for the Study of Instruction. *Rational Planning in Curriculum and Instruction.* Washington: National Education Association, 1967.

15. Nixon, John E., and Ann E. Jewett. *Physical Education Curriculum,* New York: Ronald Press, 1964.

16. Pelton, Barry C. *New Curriculum Perspectives.* Dubuque, Iowa: W. C. Brown, 1970.

17. Phillips, James A., Jr. "General Trends in Curriculum Development Today," *The Ohio High School Athlete* (May 1968), pp. 207-209.

18. Simpson, Elizabeth J. *The Classification of Educational Objectives: Psychomotor Domain.* Urbana: University of Illinois Press, 1966.

19. Taba, Hilda. *Curriculum Development.* New York: Harcourt, Brace and World, 1962.

20. Vogel, Paul. "Battle Creek Physical Education Curriculum Project," *Journal of Health, Physical Education and Recreation* (September 1969), pp. 25-29.

the school program in physical education

chapter 4

*Acceptance of all the traditional patterns of education
makes practitioners in any field unresponsive to needed
changes and perpetuates concepts and practices that
are no longer useful.*

MARLIN M. MACKENZIE

Physical education today is characterized by exciting, dramatic, and almost constant changes. However, it can be said with more than a fair degree of accuracy that the "typical" school program in physical education is not difficult to describe. As a matter of fact, the former Superintendent of Schools of the state of California quite accurately stated that the physical education class in most high schools is characterized by taking attendance, checking out a bunch of balls to a bunch of kids, and telling them to play the game.[1] Any criticism by the authors of current programs is not meant to disparage the teachers or the schools; rather, our purpose is to draw attention to the great need for change.

The study of curriculum and its attendant development of a school program typically begins at the upper-division undergraduate or graduate level. Therefore it is not the intent of this chapter to develop curriculum makers at the beginning of professional study. We feel, however, that an early exposure to curricular concepts and program building will motivate the student to recognize the need for further, detailed study in this area.

AIMS AND OBJECTIVES

Traditionally, physical education has attempted to be all things to all people. Almost regardless of stated educational objectives, physical educators industriously tried to prove how they could teach toward them. In fact, physical education was so involved in being "educational" that it seemed to overlook what its unique concerns *ought* to be. As pointed out in the last chapter, this situation is changing as theorists wrestle with curricular concepts. We can hope, as the theorists construct conceptual curricula, that the practitioners will change teaching procedures to keep pace. A recent issue of *Quest* deals exclusively and cogently with this concern.[2]

There is rather strong agreement today that the focus of the discipline of physical education is human movement. It therefore seems logical that the aim of this area of study is to produce a person who uses his body efficiently and effectively in all movement patterns because he has a cognitive understanding of movement, as well as an affective appreciation of the value of purposeful movement.

Although objectives can be stated in many different ways, there is a definite trend today toward stating them as behavioral outcomes. The beginning professional student in physical education will be introduced further to these

---

1. Max L. Rafferty, Jr., "A Critical Look at Physical Education," *California Journal of Secondary Education*, 33 (January 1958), p. 32.

2. "Educational Changes in the Teaching of Physical Education," *Quest,* Monograph 15 (January 1971).

various ways when he is exposed to methodology and pedagogy. Statements of objectives can be found in almost any textbook, any syllabus, or any course of study. One of the criticisms leveled against writers of objectives is that such statements are generally elusive, if not illusory, and therefore of little value to the teacher. Esbensen[3] says that a well-stated objective needs to define what a student will be able to do under what conditions and to what extent.

1. "The student should have an adequate comprehension of the principles of movement." No one would quarrel with this statement, but it does not tell us what the student should be able to *do* as a result of this "comprehension," nor does it define the *condition* of "adequate."

2. "The student should be able to use the vocabulary of basic movement so that he can act appropriately to verbal stimuli." This statement defines a *condition* of "verbal stimuli," but it does not mention to what *extent* the child should be able to use movement vocabulary.

3. "The student should be able to traverse within ten seconds a twenty-foot obstacle course while manipulating a ball." This statement delineates performance, extent, and a condition.

4. "Children need to learn to accept responsibility." This statement, though no doubt true, is not expressed in terms of a behavioral outcome, nor does it meet any of Esbensen's criteria.

Regardless of the manner in which objectives are stated, the following are most often properly considered to be physical education objectives.

1. *Organic development or physical fitness.* Many physical educators describe this objective as being the most important one. Whether one agrees or not, it cannot be denied that physical education is the only school program concerned with the development of strength, endurance, and other attributes of physical fitness.

2. *Skill development.* Neuromuscular coordination and the development and refinement of movement and activity skills are certainly also unique to physical education.

3. *Emotional health.* If one learns specific activity skills well so that he can engage in some of the "lifetime sports" during his leisure time, he is more apt to be able to cope with the pressures of everyday living.

---

3. Thorwald Esbensen, "Writing Educational Objectives," *Phi Delta Kappan,* 48 (January 1967), pp. 246-247.

4. *Mental development.* Awareness and understanding of the principles of movement constitute but one example of how physical education can contribute to the "mental development" of the child.

5. *Social development.* Desirable attitudes, such as courage, sharing, fair play, and concern for one's fellowman, can be fostered in a properly conducted program of physical education.

A great many educational theorists today propose that objectives for the students, as expressed by them, should also be considered in any planning for instruction. Such objectives typically include the following.

1. To develop a positive self-concept.

2. To be accepted as a member of a group or team.

3. To increase enjoyment in sports participation through skill refinement.

4. To relax and forget study pressures.

All of the objectives above are appropriate to physical education, and the manner in which the individual instructor deals with them will no doubt be determined by his value system. Table 4.1 shows a well-known ordered and logical arrangement of objectives.[4] Note that the hierarchy follows rather closely those concepts of aims and objectives previously discussed. The ultimate aim is philosophic, and its complete attainment is at best difficult. The objectives range from remote (general) to immediate (specific), and they are finally expressed as outcomes (behavioral goals).

It is doubtful that any attempt at arranging a hierarchy of objectives, whether from the instructor's or from the student's viewpoint, would be entirely acceptable. Thus the importance of the value judgment underlying educational concerns is apparent. According to Brackenbury,[5] educators must turn to philosophers for help in determining those values important in a democratic society. Unfortunately, philosophers seem to have abrogated that responsibility, and thus there is confusion about desired goals for education. Philosophy and education must work together and become mutually reconstructive if education is to become more meaningful.[6]

---

4. Karl W. Bookwalter, *Physical Education in the Secondary Schools* (Washington: Center for Applied Research in Education, 1964), p. 13.

5. Robert L. Brackenbury, "Guidelines to Help Schools Formulate and Validate Objectives," in *Rational Planning in Curriculum and Instruction* (Washington: National Education Association, 1967), pp. 89-108.

6. Charles J. Brauner and Hobert W. Burns, *Problems in Education and Philosophy* (Englewood Cliffs, N.J.: Prentice-Hall, 1965), p. 20.

TABLE 4.1. THE PURPOSES OF PHYSICAL EDUCATION

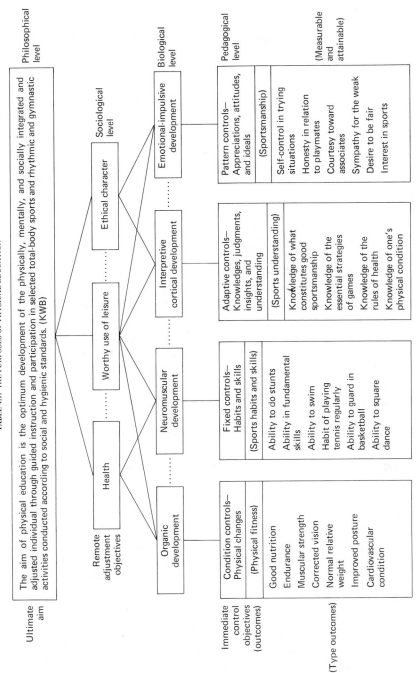

CURRICULUM IN PHYSICAL EDUCATION

Although the curriculum includes more than the formal course of study, when one considers the program of activities in a particular subject area, he is usually thinking in terms of curriculum.

La Porte's classic, *Physical Education Curriculum,*[7] presents a "carefully graded curriculum" which serves two purposes: (1) to set standards in physical education, and (2) to unify programs so that children can transfer from school to school without losing continuity in instruction. This treatise, originally published in 1937, has undergone several revisions, the latest by Cooper in 1968. It is not surprising that a study attempting to achieve the purposes stated above tends to be overstructured. Although the authors state that the suggested percentages of time for particular types of activity are only approximate and that the listed activities are merely samplings, there are invariably some teachers and supervisors who must "go by the book." Under such circumstances, the program immediately loses sight of its product, the individual child. Tables 4.2, 4.3, and 4.4 are reproductions of the sample programs advocated by LaPorte and his associates. So long as the professional student uses them in the manner intended, they can be beneficial in program planning.

As mentioned before, the greatest drawback in listing activities in tabular form, along with suggested time allotments for each, is the apparent lack of concern for the learner. Critics of education today constantly decry the "dehumanizing" process that is carried on in "joyless" schools.[8] The trend toward movement education, as discussed in Chapter 5, along with its attendant methodology, represents a significant attempt to make the learner the core of the educative process. Mosston's[9] plea for changing teaching techniques in physical education so that the individual learner is not subjugated to the group is being heard by more and more concerned teachers of physical education.

Tables 4.5 and 4.6 present a "program" of activities from a movement education viewpoint for grades kindergarten to six. Notice that each triangular dimension overlaps the others and that the entire program is ostensibly less highly structured than those shown in Tables 4.2, 4.3, and 4.4. Table 4.6 includes primarily the psychomotor and cognitive domains; Table 4.5 includes the affective domain as well.

A perusal of the different tables in this chapter may confuse the student, since they seem to indicate a lack of consensus among curriculum makers as to exactly what should be included in a program of activities at a particular level.

7. William Ralph La Porte (revised by John M. Cooper, Indiana University), *The Physical Education Curriculum* (Los Angeles: College Book Store, 1968).

8. Charles Silberman, *Crisis in the Classroom* (New York: Random House, 1970).

9. Muska Mosston, *Teaching Physical Education: From Command to Discovery* (Columbus, Ohio: Charles E. Merrill, 1966).

TABLE 4.2 SAMPLE PROGRAM FOR THE PRIMARY LEVEL (GRADES 1-3)

1. *Fundamental Movements* **20%**
   Locomotor: walking, running, skipping, galloping, whirling, swaying.
   Axial: swinging, sustaining, etc.

2. *Rhythmic Activities* (could be combined with locomotor activities if music
   accompaniment is used): **20%**
   Farmer in the Dell, Looby Loo, Mulberry Bush, Chimes of Dunkirk, Old
   Roger is Dead, The Swing, Carrousel, Jolly is the Miller, Oats, peas, beans, etc.

3. *Games* **30%**
   Simple chasing games such as cat and mice, Jack be nimble, squirrel in trees,
   cat and rat, hound and rabbit, midnight, lame fox and chickens, etc.
   Athletic games such as boundary ball, dodge ball, hand polo, kick ball, bound
   ball.

4. *Self-Testing Activities* **30%**
   Duck walk, rabbit hop, human rocker, crab walk, forward roll, frog hand
   stand, etc.

5. *Relays* (part of games and/or self-testing section)
                                                              Total 100%
   Swimming should be offered here if a pool is available.

Note: Descriptions of above typical activities will be found in most game books and
elementary school manuals. The activities listed are merely samplings.

The time allotments indicated in percentages are approximate, merely to indicate the relative
importance. These will vary somewhat with grade—relays receiving emphasis from the second
grade on, and athletic games from the third grade on. In many cases the activities included
under the several headings will be selected from the subject matter of a given *unit of work* or
center of interest around which the entire program of a given grade may be centered. It is very
important that the physical education activities be integrated with the rest of the program of
this level.

William Ralph La Porte, *The Physical Education Curriculum,* revised by John M. Cooper,
Indiana University (Los Angeles: College Book Store, 1968), p. 29.

Quite so! Indeed, it would be unrealistic to expect complete agreement on such a
complex topic, because each teacher, as an individual, has a philosophy of
physical education uniquely his own. For example, note that Table 4.2 indicates
that children in grades 1-3 should receive approximately 20 percent of their total
physical education instructional time in rhythmic activities, and the table lists
several examples of singing games, such as "Farmer in the Dell" and "Looby
Loo." However, the instructor who teaches from the movement education
perspective (see Chapter 5) would first proclaim that 20 percent of the total
instructional time is far too little for rhythms at the primary level, and he would
also decry the lack of opportunity for children to be creative in such a
structured activity as "Farmer in the Dell." Conversely, the instructor who is not
movement-education-oriented is not likely to be easily convinced that the

TABLE 4.3 SAMPLE PROGRAM FOR THE ELEMENTARY LEVEL (GRADES 4-6)

1. *Games* 50%
   Athletic games
   > *Basketball type:* captain ball, captain basketball, corner ball, line basketball, nine-court basketball, newcomb, six-court basketball, six-hole basketball, quadruple dodge ball.
   > *Softball type:* bombardment, bat ball, circle strike, end ball, fongo, hit pin baseball, long ball, one and two old cat, triangle ball, and work up.
   > *Soccer type:* advancement, circle soccer, corner kick ball, field ball, kick ball, punt back, rotation soccer, simplified soccer, soccer dodge ball, and soccer keep away.
   > *Volleyball type:* bound ball, feather ball, net ball, schoolroom volleyball, and sponge ball.

   Chasing games
   > Bears and cattle, circle chase, gathering sticks, two and three deep, catch of fish, last man, pom pom pullaway, all stand, club snatch, cross tag, dare base, duck on a rock, prisoner's base, etc.

2. *Rhythmical Activities* 20%
   > Broom dance, Dutch couple dance, Pop goes the Weasel, Bleking, Virginia Reel, Sellengers Round, Ace of Diamonds, Gustaf's Skoal, Seven Jumps, Norwegian Mountain March, Lottie is Dead, etc.

3. *Self-Testing* 30%
   > *Events:* Batting for accuracy, base running, baseball throw for accuracy, basketball pass for accuracy—for goal—for distance, pull up, push up, broad jump, high jump, soccer kick for goal—for distance, etc.
   > *Stunts:* Head stand, forward roll, backward roll, cartwheel, heel click, wooden man, jump the stick, Indian wrestle, Eskimo roll, front foot flip, knee and toe wrestle, hand wrestle, knee spring elephant walk, triple roll, etc.

4. *Relays* (Part of games and/or self-testing sections)
   > Arch ball relay, hopping relay, stunt relays, all-up Indian club relay, over and under relay, shuttle relay, stride ball relay, skin the snake relay, etc.

5. *Inclement Weather Activities* (Games that may be conducted in the classroom.)

Total 100%

Note: Descriptions of the above typical activities can be found in most game books and elementary school manuals. The activities listed are merely samplings.

The time allotments in percentages are approximate, to suggest relative importance. The selection of activities as in the primary level should be adapted closely to the *center of interest or culture area* being studied at the time in a given grade. It is suggested that the self-testing events be practiced as an integral part of the corresponding game and that many of the relays be composed of elements of the same game. Tumbling stunts should be kept very simple, and rhythmical activities should include good variety. In all activities strong emphasis should be placed on proper *body mechanics,* and on *fundamental skills* of running, jumping, throwing, catching, striking, kicking, etc.

William Ralph La Porte, *The Physical Education Curriculum,* revised by John M. Cooper, Indiana University (Los Angeles: College Book Store, 1968), p. 30.

TABLE 4.4 SAMPLE PROGRAM FOR THE JUNIOR HIGH SCHOOL
(GRADES 7-9) AND SENIOR HIGH SCHOOL (GRADES 10-12)

	Boys Weeks	Girls Weeks	Boys Weeks	Girls Weeks
1. *Survival and Water Safety* Swimming — Diving — Life Saving . .	18	18	12	12
2. *Dancing and Rhythms* Folk — Square — Social — Modern (Girls)	12	18	12	18
3. *Team Sports* a) *Court and Diamond Games* Volleyball — Softball — Basketball — 2-Court Basketball (Junior High Girls)	18	18	12	12
b) *Field Sports* Soccer — Speedball — Touch Football (Boys) — Fieldball (Junior High Girls) — Field Hockey (Senior High Girls)	18	12	18	12
4. *Tumbling Gymnastics* Tumbling — Pyramids — Apparatus — Relays — Stunts — Body Mechanics and Body Building — Endurance and strength	12	12	12	12
5. *Individual and Dual Sports* a) Tennis — Badminton — Handball or Golf or Archery	12	12	30[*]	30[*]
b) *Additional Sports and Activities* selected from the following list: Boating and canoeing — Bowling — Bowling — Hiking and Camping — Horseshoes — Fencing — Fly and Bait Casting — Paddle Tennis — Riding — Skating — Snowshoeing — Squash — Table Tennis — Trampoline — Weight Training — Outdoor Education — Wrestling; or, devote more time to dual activities listed under "a" but many should be in co-educational activities	18	18	12	12
	Total of 108 Weeks		Total of 108 Weeks	

Notes on p. 48.

[*]Some choice permitted where feasible.

Notes to Table 4.4

The time allotments are approximate in terms of relative values, and are subject to minor adjustment. They are listed in terms of weeks. A given activity can be concentrated in one year with a specific number of weeks or it may be split between two of the three years or distributed equally between the three years according to preference of a given school. If desired it is possible to schedule the activities to fit seasonal sports.

It is understood that this schedule is for class instruction purposes, to be supplemented by an opportunity for extensive intramural participation by all students. Where this extra laboratory period is not available, the last third or fourth part of the regular class period should be devoted to enthusiastic participation in the activity or game being studied. In any case, sufficient participation should be given in the class period to assure adequate motivation and appreciation of the game as a unified whole.

It is recommended that in connection with all activities, basic instruction and guidance be given in fundamental body mechanics, the efficient use of the body as a coordinated unit. The most effective instruction in the proper handling of the body probably comes from good example plus repeated cautioning on how to hold and to use the body in a variety of situations—functional posture. This involves the development of both protective skills and expressive skills.

It is recommended that each activity be given continuously for at least six weeks, at the senior high level. This would mean that the class instruction in a given activity such as basketball would appear in only one of the three years of the senior high. A student should have opportunity, however, for additional participation in the intramural program or the interschool team program.

William Ralph La Porte, *The Physical Education Curriculum,* revised by John M. Cooper (Los Angeles: College Book Store, 1968), pp. 31-32.

approach shown in Tables 4.5 and 4.6 allows sufficient time to develop specialized sports skills. Thus it once again becomes apparent that attention to philosophic bases underlying activity programs is of prime importance.

SUMMARY

Education today professes a belief in individual expression, self-control, and self-actualization. The school program in physical education will more nearly embrace these concepts—in theory as well as in practice—as physical educators pay more attention to the delineation of objectives based on individual needs and the subsequent formulation of programs which will best meet these objectives.

TABLE 4.5 MODEL OF DEVELOPMENTAL PHASES RELATED TO MOVEMENT EXPERIENCES

Movement Experiences / Developmental Phases

Early Phase	Subsequent Phase	Later Phase	Late Phase
Awareness	*Fundamental Skills*	*Specialized Skills*	*Movement (Skill) Specialization*
Self: body parts movement potential Kinesthesia	Proficiency Appropriate use of body parts. Combinations of movement.	Effective combinations of movement elements and fundamental motor skills. Quality and purpose. Movement commonalities in selected specialized skills.	Utilization of related components of previous phases. Skill in perception of intra and interdisciplinary relationships.
Environment: changes, limitations, possibilities			
Self Confidence	*Self Understanding*	*Self Evaluation*	*Self-Actualization*
Movement Control Achievement Acceptance	Differentiation between importance of self and group. Desire and ability to control movement. Body structure and movement potential.	Critical evaluation of movement. Body potential for achieving excellence in specific form. Acceptance. Realistic view of achievement.	Establishing own value system Discrete quality of self-discipline Acceptance of self, capacities, worth
Habits of Thought	*Habits of Thought*	*Habits of Thought*	*Habits of Thought*
Movement vocabulary Kinesthetic, Verbal Selection of appropriate movements to solve problems	Significance of proficiency. Relationship of movement results to principles of human movement. Importance of effective group action. Relationship between movement elements, body, and fundamental motor skills.	Decision making—selection of appropriate movement combinations, strategy applied through movement contributes to control of self and environment; to feeling of worth and power over self. Valuing movement. Relationship of mechanical laws of motion to principles of human movement.	Continuous modification and application of ideas for productive change.

Courtesy of Naomi Allenbaugh, Assistant Director, School of Health, Physical Education and Recreation, Ohio State University.

TABLE 4.6 MODEL FOR MOVEMENT EXPERIENCES FOUNDATIONAL TO SPECIALIZED

Movement Tasks Based on Content Involving:	Fundamental Motor Skill Tasks designed for study of:	Specialized Motor Skills Tasks designed for study of:	Specialization in Selected Activity Skills toward "championship" performance:
1. Movement elements space, force, time, flow and their dimensions	3. Locomotor skills 4. Non-locomotor skills 5. Manipulative skills and the	Sequences of movement using fundamental motor skills and movement elements designed to achieve a specific purpose in a particular activity:	High level of movement proficiency in skill sequences. Use of movement commonalities; application of movement patterns, space-force-time factors, strategies, etc.
2. Body Focus Relationships Leads Support Transfer of weight Control	6. Principles of Human Movement (Follow through) (Opposition) (Objective Focus) (Total Assembly)	Forms of More Complex Traditional Activities: games, sports, dance, gymnastics, aquatics	*Habits of Thought* Application of knowledge and Kinesthesia (feedback) for movement evaluation and improvement.
Simple Form: Traditional Activities— games, dance gymnastics, aquatics, utilizing knowledges and skills derived from 1 and 2 above	*Modified Forms:* Traditional Activities— games, dance gymnastics, aquatics utilizing knowledges and skills derived from 1, 2, 3, 4, 5, 6	*Mechanical Laws of Motion* Gravity Leverage Equilibrium Force Rebound Spin	Decision-making.

Physical Education Content Knowledge and Skills

Courtesy of Naomi Allenbaugh, Assistant Director, School of Health, Physical Education and Recreation, Ohio State University.

STUDENT PROJECTS

1. Review several books in physical education which list objectives, particularly those which deal with curriculum. List the similarities and contrasts in objectives and attempt to explain why they exist.
2. What percentage of the objectives above meet the criteria of performance, condition, and extent?
3. Conduct an informal survey among a sampling of students living in residence halls to determine the program of activities they had in their high school physical education programs. Include information on the approximate amount of time spent on each.

GLOSSARY OF TERMS

Philosophy of education   An area of systematic study which attempts to guide educational theory and practice.

Behavioral outcomes   Objectives or goals for any course of study expressed in terms of desired behavior.

Review all the terms listed for Chapter 3.

SELECTED REFERENCES

1. Bookwalter, Karl W. *Physical Education in the Secondary Schools.* Washington: Center for Applied Research in Education, 1964.
2. Brackenbury, Robert L. "Guidelines to Help Schools Formulate and Validate Objectives," in *Rational Planning in Curriculum and Instruction.* Washington: National Education Association, 1967.
3. Brauner, Charles J., and Hobert W. Burns. *Problems in Education and Philosophy.* Englewood Cliffs, N.J.: Prentice-Hall, 1965.
4. "Educational Change in the Teaching of Physical Education," *Quest,* Monograph 15 (January 1971).
5. Esbensen, Thorwald. "Writing Educational Objectives," *Phi Delta Kappan,* **48** (January 1967).
6. La Porte, William Ralph. *The Physical Education Curriculum,* Los Angeles: College Book Store, 1968.
7. Mager, Robert F. *Preparation Objectives for Programmed Instruction.* San Francisco: Fearon Press, 1962.
8. Mosston, Muska. *Teaching Physical Education: From Command to Discovery.* Columbus, Ohio: Charles E. Merrill, 1966.

9. Rafferty, Max L., Jr. "A Critical Look at Physical Education." *California Journal of Secondary Education,* **33** (January 1958).

10. Silberman, Charles. *Crisis in the Classroom.* New York: Random House, 1970.

11. Taba, Hilda. *Curriculum Development: Theory and Practice.* New York: Harcourt, Brace and World, 1962.

movement education

chapter 5

*Every new movement or manifestation of human
activity, when unfamiliar to people's minds, is sure to
be misrepresented and misunderstood.*

EDWARD CARPENTER

Movement education has perhaps been the most noteworthy trend in physical education in the United States in the past decade, if not in this century. And as suggested in the quotation above, it has been widely misrepresented and just as widely misunderstood. The quandary regarding the "movement movement" is due to several factors. Since the methodology of movement education consists largely of problem-solving, many critics of the movement see in it a regression to the throw-the-ball-out-and-let-them-go-at-it type of "instruction" that has been all too prevalent in the field. Some of the confusion is due to semantics, some to ignorance of the movement, some to the lack of agreement among those who profess to be experts in the area, and some to the fact that too enthusiastic advocates have made unwarranted claims for it and have thereby isolated potential supporters who prefer more tangible proof before they embrace what may be just another fad. What follows is an attempt to describe objectively the history of movement education as a curriculum—its purposes, its program, its justification, and its probable future.

Children learn to move; children move to learn. Photo courtesy of Heidie Mitchell, Department of Physical Education for Women, Kent State University.

HISTORY

Movement education received an impetus in Great Britain in the 1940's and earlier, when there arose a new conception of human movement, revolving at least partially around the work of Rudolf Laban, a dancer and choreographer, and his theory of movement analysis based on *what* moves, *how* it moves, *where* it moves, and what the relationship of the movement with other moving and nonmoving factors is. *Educational gymnastics,* the term used in the British movement, has as its objective the teaching of efficient body movement through a skillful combination of movements in relation to space, force, time, and flow, the commonly accepted *elements of movement.*[1] The program is characterized by movement exploration, great quantities of equipment, creative teaching, and less structured lessons. In addition to fostering skill in managing the body in a variety of circumstances, the program stresses cognitive aspects of movement since the body cannot be trained in a vacuum. The affective domain also receives emphasis as youngsters experience in and through movement a concern for others, a growing sense of confidence with an attendant lessening of self-consciousness, and an awareness of pleasureful activity as skill levels increase. Thus the three classifications of educational objectives, as discussed in Chapter 3, can be met in a program of movement education. As more and more American teachers of physical education observed these British gymnastics lessons, noting the methodology employed and the good results obtained, they became extremely interested in exploration as a method for teaching movement. The seed of what was to become the movement education program in the schools of the United States was being planted.

It is of interest to note, however, that since the 1920's such American leaders as Thomas Wood, Rosalind Cassidy, and Jesse Feiring Williams have been proposing concepts of physical education which now fall under the general rubric of movement education. In the 1930's a pioneer leader in dance, Margaret H'Doubler, proposed new concepts in dance and applied them to basic movement. These forward-looking educators were even then attempting to apply research findings in child growth and development and the behavioral sciences to physical education.[2]

Nevertheless, it was not until after World War II that international exchange programs and Anglo-American workshops in elementary school physical education served as the catalyst for the growing trend toward acceptance of movement education as a vital part of the school program in physical education in this

---

1. W. McD. Cameron and Peggy Pleasance, *Education in Movement* (Oxford: Basil Blackwell, 1964), p. 4.

2. Elizabeth A. Ludwig, "Toward an Understanding of Basic Movement Education in the Elementary Schools," *JOHPER,* **39** (March 1968), pp. 26-27.

country. No doubt the effectiveness of the catalyst was increased by such factors as the apparent novelty of the approach to the education of the whole child, a growing dissatisfaction with elementary school physical education programs and their sports and games orientation, which left many youngsters woefully inadequate insofar as physical skill was concerned, and last but far from least, the theories advanced by some psychologists and educators that motor learnings, as the earliest learnings of the child, form the base from which all other learnings occur. Several kinds of therapy programs to aid youngsters with perceptual-motor defects (advocated by Kephart,[3] Doman,[4] Delacato,[5] and Fostig,[6] among others) have gained varying degrees of acceptance among educators and medical men.

THE PROGRAM TODAY

Although movement education as a curricular program is now hardly a new idea in the field of physical education, recurring questions among those in the profession indicate that confusion still exists about the purpose of the program, the definition of some of its specific terminology, and its place in the total spectrum of elementary school physical education.

If physical education is an academic discipline, then the conceptual approach to teaching is indicated. One of the most respected authorities in the field of elementary school physical education in this country states: "Physical education, like every other discipline, can be organized so each child can gradually develop the main ideas of the discipline through the accumulation, comprehension, and synthesis of the related subject matter."[7] She then discusses three of the many concepts around which physical education can be organized.

1. Man moves to survive. This concept revolves around the "anatomical and physiological nature of man and his need to acquire physiological understanding and readiness for efficient movement."[8]

---

3. D. H. Radler and Newell C. Kephart, *Success Through Play* (New York: Harper and Row, 1961).

4. Glenn Doman, *How to Teach Your Baby to Read.* (New York: Random House, 1964).

5. Carl Delacato, *The Diagnosis and Treatment of Speech and Reading Problems* (Springfield, Ill.: Charles C. Thomas, 1963).

6. Marianne Frostig and David Horn, *The Frostig Program for the Development of Visual Perception* (Chicago: Follett, 1964).

7. Naomi Allenbaugh, "Learning about Movement," *NEA Journal,* 56 (March 1967), p. 48.

8. *Ibid.*

Body awareness—moving the hula hoop with different parts of the body. Photo courtesy of Lorie Coll and Ravenna (Ohio) City School System.

2. Man moves to discover and understand his environment. "As a child comes to understand his environment and use it successfully in movement, he acquires a more realistic body image and a more wholesome self-concept."[9]

3. Man moves to control and adjust to his environment. As the child learns better to understand both himself and his environment, he realizes that the ability to "control and adjust" is based on efficient movement. "Thus he begins to work for the advantageous use of the elements of movement—space, time, force, and flow."[10]

_____

9. *Ibid.*
10. *Ibid.*

With this conceptual approach, the purpose of movement education seems inextricably woven around what movement educators call *body management*—the ability of the child to *control* his body in movement patterns because he *understands* the way his body can move in relation to the many forces exerted upon it.

Movement education is the term used to describe that part of the physical education curriculum which aims to achieve this purpose,[11] whereas *basic movement* refers to the content of the program, namely, an emphasis on gross motor skills, both locomotor and nonlocomotor, in relation to the elements of movement: force, flow, time, and space.

Movement exploration, the *method* used for teaching body management, is characterized by two main approaches, problem-solving and guided discovery. The problem-solving approach is best described as an effort by the teacher to design a problem in such a manner that the youngster, through experimentation, discovers for himself the best and most efficient movement pattern. *Guided discovery* is also problem-solving, but the teacher plays a more direct role in that she poses the problem in such a manner that certain desired outcomes are likely.

In both of these approaches, the teacher is more than an interested observer. She actively teaches throughout the lesson. Although she does not demonstrate how particular movements should be performed, she helps children evaluate, she helps them understand why certain movements feel more comfortable, and she can suggest possible changes.

The physical educator who is used to the traditional program in physical education at the elementary school level is often concerned about the refinement of skills necessary for specific sports, games, and dance. The movement education approach does not disregard such skill formation. (Refer again to Table 4.6.) Rather, the curriculum in movement education focuses on basic movement as the foundation on which fundamental skills are built. The transition from the fundamental skills to specific sports skills should then evolve not only more quickly but with a greater degree of perfection.

Not only the "traditionalist" in physical education but also the classroom teacher is often concerned about the paucity of structured game situations in a movement education program. Their concern is perhaps lessened when the movement educator explains that an analysis of most games reveals how space- and boundary-oriented they are, how many obstacles there are to overcome, how necessary it is to be aware of the directions in which one may move, how many different pathways can be taken to reach the goal, and how many

11. Lorena Porter, *Movement Education for Children* (Washington: American Association of Elementary-Kindergarten-Nursery Educators, 1969) p. 5.

different levels there are at which movement occurs. Understanding this, one can see that if the child is well instructed in a good movement education program during his early experience with organized physical education, not only will he have the body management necessary for more effective refinement of sports skills at a later date, but he should also avoid some of the trauma and disappointment too often associated with the traditional method of teaching sports and games. Most of the rules and techniques in a typical sport such as basketball far exceed a child's ability to cope with them. Through movement education, with its emphasis on basic movement, a child should better learn to adjust to the constantly changing environment found in games. Success, a positive reinforcer, is thus more apt to be an outcome.[12]

The methodology of movement education is not restricted to the elementary school physical education program. Although physical educators have for years been advocating the teaching of motor skills with an application of mechanical principles, few of them are well-versed in the problem-solving approach. Therefore, their efforts have been mostly limited to teacher-directed goals. It seems clear, however, that more and more teachers at both the secondary and college level are experimenting with an approach to the teaching of sports and dance that encourages the learner to help set his own goals. Empirical data regarding the effectiveness of the problem-solving approach are becoming more available as college researchers attempt to discover and qualify the differences in results accruing from different teaching styles. For the most part, such studies tend to show the superiority of the problem-solving approach to teaching over the traditional method. Selected studies are cited in footnotes 13-17. The prospective teacher is urged to read carefully as many of them as possible. (All of the cited theses are available on microcards.) Russell's study is particularly interesting in that the results indicate that the "traditional" approach may even influence *skilled* performers negatively.

---

12. Heidie Mitchell, Unpublished lecture notes, PE 241, Kent State University, 1970.

13. Iris L. Garland, *Effectiveness of Problem-Solving Method in Learning Swimming,* unpublished master's thesis, University of California, Los Angeles, 1960.

14. Gayle Gravelee, *A Comparison of the Effectiveness of Two Methods of Teaching a Four-Week Unit on Selected Motor Skills to First Grade Children,* unpublished master's thesis, University of North Carolina, Greensboro, 1965.

15. Marilyn R. Russell, *Effectiveness of Problem-Solving Methods in Learning a Gross Motor Skill,* unpublished master's thesis, University of Washington, 1967.

16. Martha Van Allen, *An Investigation Using the Movement Exploration Approach in the Teaching of Selected Swimming and Diving Skills,* unpublished doctoral dissertation, Springfield College, 1966.

17. Yvonne Zeigler, *A Comparison of Two Methods of Teaching Gymnastics,* unpublished master's thesis, University of Wisconsin, 1965.

THE FUTURE OF MOVEMENT EDUCATION

There has been widespread dissatisfaction with the program of physical education in the schools today. The "movement movement" is undoubtedly one expression of this dissatisfaction as physical educators come to grips with poor programs, poor teaching, and poor attempts at conceptually organizing a body of knowledge revolving around human movement.

Whether the program of movement education, as described, is a passing fancy or an effective means toward the end of physically educated, self-directed, well-functioning human beings is, of course, still a matter of conjecture. It seems quite clear, however, that the program is gaining strength, particularly at the elementary school level. It also seems very clear that the ultimate worth of the program depends on the strength of the teachers in it. Unless a teacher truly understands the concepts underlying the discipline of physical education, he cannot master the exceptionally creative approach demanded and consequently cannot be effective in teaching. A very comprehensive recent treatment of both the content and the pedagogical implication of movement education, by Gilliom[18], should prove of inestimable help to the student or teacher who seeks to understand in greater depth this phase of the total physical education program.

Evaluation of the child in a movement education program, except subjectively and in relation only to himself, is of little concern to the movement educator, who considers as one of the strengths of the program the fact that there is no single criterion of correct movement. Therefore the child experiences only success. Of course, he can be guided to greater success by the teacher who understands how the child's body can most efficiently move within its own unique physical structure. However, evaluation of the *program* needs greater attention and a more sustained focus. Until movement educators can come up with more empirical evidence supporting some of their claims, it seems unlikely that universal acceptance will be forthcoming.

Locke[19,20] has written especially cogent critiques of movement education. His contention is that the future of movement education depends on (1) a more lucid delineation of why there continues to be dissatisfaction with the traditional program of physical education, (2) a definition of behavior-oriented objectives, (3) attention to teaching techniques, the strengths of which can be

18. Bonnie C. Gilliom, *Basic Movement Education for Children: Rationale and Teaching Units* (Reading, Mass.: Addison-Wesley, 1970).

19. Lawrence F. Locke, "Movement Education: A Description and Critique," in R. C. Brown and B. J. Cratty (eds.), *New Perspectives of Man in Action* Engelwood Cliffs, N.J.: Prentice-Hall, 1969), pp. 200-226.

20. Lawrence F. Locke, "The Movement Movement," *JOHPER,* 37 (January 1966), pp. 26-27, 73.

empirically demonstrated, and (4) the development of "well-publicized, attractive pilot programs" in the public schools that will catch the attention of school administrators, perhaps the only ones who can directly effect a change in the school curriculum.[21]

There seems to be little disagreement with the position that human movement must be the focus of the discipline.

> Since movement is used in some way, to some degree, in almost every task accomplished by human beings, the teaching of efficient movement becomes both an obligation and a challenge—a challenge to help each student develop the ability to use his body effectively in the performance of all tasks demanded of it, whether these tasks involve everyday living skills, work skills, or recreational skills.[22]

The proverbial writing on the wall has never been clearer. The very survival of the physical education program depends on the ability of the discipline to translate the writing into unified, defensible action.

---

21. *Ibid.,* p. 73.
22. Marion R. Broer, *Efficiency of Human Movement* (Philadelphia: W. B. Saunders, 1966), p. 363.

STUDENT PROJECTS

1. Prepare an oral or written report on the studies cited in footnotes 13-17.
2. Search out empirical studies dealing with the perceptual-motor therapy programs cited in footnotes 3-6.
3. Review *Promising Practices in Elementary School Physical Education* (See 2, References), and report on the scope of professional assistance and material available to the elementary school physical education teacher.
4. Visit an elementary school in which the movement approach is now used. Record observed sessions.
5. Interview classroom teachers in the same elementary school. How do they compare the effectiveness of this type of curriculum with that of the "traditional" curriculum of games and sports, as reflected by the youngsters' learning in physical education.
6. If possible, talk with some of the youngsters involved in a movement education curriculum to ascertain the depth and kinds of understandings of human movement they possess.

GLOSSARY OF TERMS

Movement education That part of the physical education curriculum which aims to help the child achieve body management through an understanding of the elements of movement and the ways in which they affect his body in motion.

Body management The ability of the child to control his body as it moves.

Elements of movement Space, force, time, and flow.

>   **Space** The area in which movement occurs.
>
>   **Force** The effort required to move.
>
>   **Time** The speed with which movement occurs.
>
>   **Flow** The sequential connection of moving body parts.

Basic movement The content of the movement education program, with emphasis on gross motor skills, both locomotor and nonlocomotor.

Movement exploration The method in movement education, which employs two main approaches: problem-solving and guided discovery.

Problem-solving An attempt by the teacher to design a problem so that the child can discover for himself, via experimentation, the most efficient movement pattern.

Guided discovery A more teacher-directed approach to problem-solving, by which an attempt is made to guarantee certain desired movement outcomes.

Conceptual approach In methodology, an attempt to foster the child's comprehension of physical education through a synthesis of accumulated subject matter.

SELECTED REFERENCES

1. Allenbaugh, Naomi. "Learning about Movement," *Journal of the National Education Associaton,* **56** (March 1967), pp. 48-51.

2. American Association for Health, Physical Education and Recreation. *Promising Practices in Elementary School Physical Education.* Washington: National Education Association, 1969.

3. Ammons, R. B., *et al.* "Long Term Retention of Perceptual Motor Skills," *Journal of Experimental Psychology,* **55** (April 1958), pp. 318-328.

4. Barrett, Kate Ross. *Exploration: A Method for Teaching Movement.* Madison, Wis.: College Printing and Typing, 1965.

5. Bilbrough, A., and P. Jones. *Physical Education in the Primary School.* London: University of London Press, 1963.

6. Bilodeau, Edward, and Ina Bilodeau. "Motor-Skills Learning: Feedback," *Annual Review of Psychology,* **12** (1961), pp. 243-259.

7. Broer, Marion R. *Efficiency of Human Movement.* Philadelphia: W. B. Saunders, 1966.

8. _____. "Movement Education: Wherein the Disagreement?" *Quest,* Monograph 2 (April 1964), pp. 19-24.

9. Brown, Camille, and Rosalind Cassidy. *Theory in Physical Education, a Guide to Program Change.* Philadelphia: Lea and Febiger, 1963.

10. Brown, Margaret C., and Betty K. Sommer. *Movement Education: Its Evolution and a Modern Approach.* Reading, Mass.: Addison-Wesley, 1969.

11. Cameron, W. McD., and Peggy Pleasance. *Education in Movement.* Oxford: Basil Blackwell, 1964.

12. Carlquist, Maja. *Rhythmical Gymnastics.* London: Methuen, 1961.

13. Delacato, Carl. *Neurological Organization and Reading.* Springfield, Ill.: Charles Thomas, 1966.

14. _____ . *The Diagnosis and Treatment of Speech and Reading Problems.* Springfield, Illinois: Charles C. Thomas, 1963.

15. Doman, Glenn. *How to Teach Your Baby to Read.* New York: Random House, 1964.

16. Engels, Virgil. "Patterned Movements: A New Justification for Physical Education," *The Physical Educator,* **25** (December 1968), pp. 170-172.

17. Espenschade, Anna S. "Perceptual-Motor Development in Children," *Acad-*

emy Papers of the American Academy of Physical Education, 1 (March 1968), pp. 14-20.

18. Frostig, Marianne, and David Horn. *The Frostig Program for the Development of Visual Perception.* Chicago: Follett, 1964.

19. Garland, Iris L. *Effectiveness of Problem-Solving Method in Learning Swimming.* Unpublished master's thesis, University of California, Los Angeles, 1960.

20. Gilliom, Bonnie C. *Basic Movement Education for Children: Rationale and Teaching Units.* Reading, Mass.: Addison-Wesley, 1970.

21. Gravelee, Gayle. *A Comparison of the Effectiveness of Two Methods of Teaching a Four-Week Unit in Selected Motor Skills to First Grade Children.* Unpublished master's thesis, University of North Carolina, Greensboro, 1965.

22. Howard, Shirley, "Movement Education Approach to Teaching in English Elementary Schools," *Journal of Health, Physical Education and Recreation,* 38 *(January 1967), pp. 30-33.*

23. Hunt, Valerie. "Movement Behavior: A Model for Action," *Quest,* Monograph 2 (April 1964), pp. 69-91.

24. Knapp, B. *Skill in Sport.* London: Routledge and Kegan Paul, 1963.

25. Laban, Rudolf, and F. C. Lawrence. *Effort.* London: MacDonald and Evans, 1947.

26. Locke, Lawrence F. "Movement Education: A Description and Critique," in R. C. Brown and B. J. Cratty (eds.), *New Perspectives of Man in Action,* Englewood Cliffs, N.J.: Prentice-Hall 1969, pp. 200-226.

27. _____. "The Movement Movement," *Journal of Health, Physical Education and Recreation,* 37 (January 1966), pp. 26-27, 73.

28. Lockhart, Aileene. "Prerequisites to Motor Learning," *Academy Papers of the American Academy of Physical Education,* 1 (March 1968), pp. 1-13.

29. Ludwig, Elizabeth A. "Toward an Understanding of Basic Movement Education in the Elementary Schools," *Journal of Health, Physical Education and Recreation,* 39 (March 1968), pp. 26-28, 77.

30. MacKenzie, Marlin M. *Toward a New Curriculum in Physical Education.* New York: McGraw-Hill, 1969.

31. Metheny, Eleanor. "How Does a Movement Mean?" *Quest,* Monograph 8 (May 1967), pp. 1-6.

32. _____. "Only by Moving Their Bodies," *Quest,* Monograph 2 (April 1964), pp. 47-51.

33. Mosston, Muska. *Developmental Movement.* Columbus, Ohio: Charles E. Merrill, 1965.

34. Piaget, Jean. *The Origins of Intelligence in Children.* New York: International Universities Press, 1966.

35. Porter, Lorena. *Movement Education for Children.* Washington: American Association of Elementary-Kindergarten-Nursery Educators, 1969.

36. *Questions and Answers about Movement Education.* ESEA—Title III Program of Movement Education for Plattsburgh (New York) Elementary Schools (Joan Tillotson, Project Director), 1968.

37. Radler, D. H., and Newell C. Kephart. *Success Through Play.* New York: Harper and Row, 1961.

38. Randall, Marjorie. *Basic Movement.* London: G. Bell, 1961.

39. Russell, Marilyn R. *Effectiveness of Problem-Solving Methods in Learning a Gross Motor Skill.* Unpublished master's thesis, University of Washington, 1967.

40. Sage, George H. *Introduction to Motor Behavior,* Reading, Mass.: Addison-Wesley, 1971.

41. Sturtevant, Mary. "Movement Efficiency and the Novice Swimmer," *The Physical Educator,* **26** (March 1969), pp. 24-25.

42. Sweeney, Robert T. *Selected Readings in Movement Education.* Reading, Mass.: Addison-Wesley, 1970.

43. Van Allen, Martha. *An Investigation Using the Movement Exploration Approach in the Teaching of Selected Swimming and Diving Skills.* Unpublished doctoral dissertation, Springfield College, 1966.

44. Zeigler, Yvonne. *A Comparison of Two Methods of Teaching Gymnastics.* Unpublished doctoral dissertation, Springfield College, 1966.

current trends in education

chapter 6

There is nothing permanent except change.

HERACLITUS

The school program in physical education encompasses the largest single application of the discipline of physical education. Consequently, those who teach physical education need always to be aware of current philosophies of education as well as the latest trends based on such philosophy. Although it is not the purpose of this chapter to discuss educational philosophy per se, the changes which are taking place in education cannot be overlooked. In their commitment to change, many administrators are encouraging teachers to be innovative and creative, and they are fostering a climate conducive to experimentation. It is up to the physical educator, then, to take advantage of such opportunities and prove once and for all that the dualism of mind and body is forever extinct, that his specialized field of learning can contribute to the objectives of all education, and that, indeed, his unique concerns are properly also concerns of all of education.

This chapter is devoted to a discussion of selected current trends in education and of ways in which these new developments can be incorporated into the teaching of physical education. No attempt is made to place a value judgment on these innovations. Only after the theorists have fully explored what "ought" to be and the teachers have shown how such findings can be put into practice, can effective evaluation take place. For most of the trends discussed, that time has not yet arrived.

TEAM TEACHING

Team teaching is a concept that has arisen as one of the many possible answers in a search for creative and better methods of instruction in American schools. The concept has been variously defined, but in general, the following criteria must be met if the effort is to be considered team teaching.

1. A corps of two or more teachers (usually at least three and no more than eight).
2. Cooperative planning, instructing, and evaluating by the corps of teachers.
3. Involvement of one or more class groups (usually more than one).
4. Consideration given to special competencies of each member of the team.
5. Designation of a team leader.
6. Flexible arrangement of facilities, equipment, and time periods.

Actually, "team organization and planning" is a more appropriate title for this educational endeavor, since it is usual at any given moment for only one individual to be teaching. Misnamed or not, the concept seems to be gaining acceptance, so an exploration of some of its characteristics is warranted.

As indicated above, a team leader is usually designated. In such a situation, the corps is considered a "hierarchical team" with a definite chain of command from top to bottom, in contrast to a "cooperative team," all of whose members share equally in responsibilities.[1] Both types of organization have advantages, but most schools report less confusion when a team leader is appointed and job descriptions are formulated. Not all teachers wish to serve on a teaching team, nor are all teachers capable of performing well as part of a team. Therefore teachers must be chosen with care, and consideration should be given to such factors as willingness to accept peer and pupil criticism, dedication to self-improvement, ability to communicate well in large groups, in-depth knowledge and skill in the area involved, and ability to use instructional media and resources to their best advantage.

Paraprofessionals can play a large role in the concept of team teaching, and flexible scheduling is undoubtedly productive of the best learning. Both of these ideas are discussed separately later in this chapter.

It seems logical to assume that the cost of team teaching is somewhat higher than that of more traditional methods of instruction, although many of its proponents claim that it is less expensive, *if properly conducted,* because large-group instruction takes care of more students at one time, less costly paraprofessionals are used to good advantage, individual study is fostered, and more efficient use of the facilities is made.

As is true with any instructional innovation, the attitude of the administration is probably the single most significant factor in the success or failure of a program. If the school principal, for example, not only is willing to try out new methods but actively encourages such experimentation on the part of his teachers, the program is likely to be successful. Obviously, such other factors as teacher interest and adequate preparation time are essential, but nothing else is so devastating as administrative apathy.

There is not an abundance of written material on team teaching in physical education; however, most authors of what material there is believe that its advantages are numerous. Among the more obvious ones are varying the teacher-pupil ratio according to the needs and abilities of the students, the competency of the teacher, and the available facilities; assigning the pupil according to his need for a particular kind of instruction; fostering professional growth among the teachers, often with greater attendant camaraderie and unification; and motivating the student to more independent study of a better quality.

It is intriguing to reflect on the fact that many of the foregoing aspects of team teaching have been practiced for many years in one part of the total physical

---

1. Judson T. Shaplin and Henry F. Olds (eds.), *Team Teaching* (New York: Harper and Row, 1964), p. 116.

education program, namely, varsity athletics. Football, for example, has often been referred to as the best-taught subject in high school. In football, the team leader (head coach) calls together the rest of his corps of teachers (assistant coaches). They cooperatively plan their instruction program, taking into consideration the special competencies of the teachers (the defensive backfield coach, for example) and the needs and abilities of the students (defensive safety players who need considerable work on pass protection). Then they set up a flexible arrangement of equipment and facilities to meet these special needs. For example, perhaps the safety men need to concentrate solely on pass protection, whereas the defensive ends need to practice rushing the quarterback. The entire teaching (coaching) team engages in cooperative evaluation of their product, and students (players) have the advantage as well as the responsibility for self-evaluation and self-improvement through the media of movies of their performance, execution charts kept by managers (paraprofessionals), instant replay television, and other means.

It is equally intriguing, as well as perplexing, to reflect on the fact that the same creative endeavors are not characteristic of the teaching in the required physical education program. The reasons are diverse, and discussion of them would require a great many pages. Perhaps the final answer lies in the fact that the typical physical educator has not "sold" his product—either to the school administration or to the public.

DIFFERENTIATED STAFFING

One of the most frequently voiced laments of teachers concerns being "freed to teach." The variety of nonteaching duties for which the typical teacher is responsible is so great that he often finds little time to prepare adequately for teaching. Then, too, there are extremely diverse teaching loads, often based on nothing more than an ill-conceived decision made a decade or two earlier. This problem is especially acute in physical education; the physical educator may have 1500 different student contacts a week, for example, whereas the mathematics teacher has "only" 600. Factors such as these underlie increasing teacher unrest and militancy.

Differentiated staffing, a concept which deals with the teacher as an individual but in an organizational context, is a "promising solution" to the problem of providing quality education by improving teacher efficiency.[2] It is predicated on the theory that the teacher is one of the most important elements in student learning and that it is at best a debilitating practice to treat all teachers

2. Fenwick English, *Et Tu, Educator, Differentiated Staffing?* (Washington: National Commission on Teacher Education and Professional Standards, National Education Association, 1969), pp. 1-5.

alike, regardless of experience or talent, insofar as instructional responsibilities, advancement, and monetary rewards are concerned. Under a plan of differentiated staffing, teachers are treated according to their ability to perform specific tasks, and they are paid according to the complexity of those tasks. Teaching thus becomes a "career," and it is possible for a dedicated teacher to plan accordingly.

Basic to any plan of differentiated staffing is the involvement of teachers in decision-making processes and in the evaluation of their colleagues. It is perhaps fair to say that many teachers in the past have not wished to be involved in either of these ventures, particularly the latter, but the pattern is changing as better prepared, more militant teachers are actively involved in every part of the entire educational program.

Rand and English[3] describe a differentiated-staffing model in which there are three basic areas of additional responsibility besides teaching: (1) "instructional management," in which a "senior teacher" functions as a learning engineer; (2) "curriculum construction," in which a "master teacher" is responsible for incorporating the latest research and educational theory into the curriculum; and (3) "staff teacher," who has advanced skill in applying research findings to the instructional act. In addition, there is an "associate teacher" category for the beginning teacher who needs to be brought along slowly under sympathetic, wise, and professional supervision.

In a program of differentiated staffing, one can apply for a position at any of the three levels described above. The acquisition of such positions is based on qualifications for the specific responsibilities involved, and contractual arrangements differ in both length and remuneration. Advancement at any level is not automatic but is based on evaluation by colleagues. Merit pay, another trend in education, is perhaps basic to this plan.

The promises of differentiated staffing for all of education, including physical education, are many. The most significant may be the opportunity for increased professionalization and a higher degree of competence in that selected personnel are freed to develop certain responsibilities and functions for the good of all teaching personnel. The end result seems almost certain to be higher-quality education for all through greater utilization of educational resources.

In physical education, one can visualize the department chairman as the master teacher, the dedicated teacher with long experience at different educational levels as the senior teacher, the teacher with a minimum of a master's degree as a staff teacher, and the beginner as the associate teacher, who,

---

3. John M. Rand and Fenwick English, "Towards a Differentiated Teaching Staff," *Phi Delta Kappan,* **49** (January 1968), pp. 264-269.

if capable and interested, cannot help growing professionally under the protection and guidance of the others.

FLEXIBLE (MODULAR) SCHEDULING

Flexible scheduling is based primarily on two concepts: (1) students with differing needs and abilities should be scheduled in classes according to these differences; and (2) not all courses need the same amount of time, and the same course may even need differing amounts of time on different occasions. For the implementation of such concepts, the school day is constructed around a specific period of time, called a module (or "mod"), which is perhaps fifteen to twenty minutes in length. The modules are then used as building blocks on which the master schedule is constructed. Whereas the traditional schedule cycles daily, the flexible schedule usually cycles weekly. Whereas the traditional schedule leaves little, if any, unscheduled time, the flexible schedule guarantees free time to the student to be used for individual study, whether preparing a "homework" assignment, practicing swimming skills, or conferring with teachers, who also have unscheduled time.

Tennis, an activity that lends itself well to coeducational instruction. Photo courtesy of the Ohio Association for Health, Physical Education and Recreation.

Four basic types of instructional groups are possible under flexible scheduling: large-group instruction, small-group instruction, independent study, and laboratory study. It is possible that most areas of instruction in physical education will use all four types in an integrated fashion. Let us say, for example, that all tenth graders, both boys and girls, meet together one day a week for two mods of large-group instruction. If their particular unit of study is tennis, they can hear lectures on the history, rules, etiquette, and training considerations for tennis, view films of tennis players in action, or hear lectures by guest tennis pros. On two other days of the week, boys and girls can meet separately or together in small groups for three or four mods of actual skill practice. On yet another day, an even smaller group that needs extra instruction because of basically poor motor skill can meet for one or two mods. In addition, the gymnasium and the tennis courts are open for independent "study"—in this case, perhaps, practice on a backboard or on a rebound net.

It is fairly easy to see how team teaching and even differentiated staffing, as discussed earlier, fit into a flexible scheduling pattern. Not all teachers are equally competent to lecture to large groups, nor do all have the patience to work with low-skilled individuals. Not all teachers have enough free time to preview movies before they are shown or to research certain sociocultural factors surrounding the game of tennis.

Flexible scheduling, like other educational innovations, does away with many traditional aspects of schooling, the elimination of which some teachers find hard to accept. For example, there are no bells to signal the beginning and end of modules; students have a great deal more freedom, and they are responsible for its wise use; emphasis is placed on performance, and it matters little whether the student learned to "perform" in a large group or in independent study; and the scheduling of time, facilities, teachers, and students is too complex to be done manually.

There are, of course, disadvantages to flexible scheduling; however, if wisely used, this concept seems to be one that is truly productive of quality education through effective use of teaching talents, through greater responsibility of the student for his own education, through more rational use of time, and through complete utilization of facilities.

THE USE OF PARAPROFESSIONALS

As mentioned earlier in this chapter, the typical teacher is faced with so many nonprofessional duties that he often has difficulty finding sufficient time to prepare adequately for instruction. Tax-conscious school patrons are beginning to realize that it is economically feasible to employ a number of paraprofessionals, sometimes called teaching aides, to perform nonteaching duties and thus to free the higher-salaried professional person to do the job for which he is most qualified.

A paraprofessional in education can be defined as a mature adult who is trained to perform various nonteaching tasks in an educational institution. The persons who may qualify are quite varied: homemakers who want only part-time jobs, college students who are helping to finance their education, retired persons who are interested in "keeping in touch" with youth and their education, and others. The tasks they can be trained to perform include typing, filing, recording test scores, issuing locks and lockers, taking attendance, supervising playground and recess activities, caring for and repairing equipment, constructing bulletin boards, showing audiovisual aids, and *assisting* in instruction.

Two criteria in the definition of a paraprofessional cannot be emphasized too strongly. First, a "mature adult" is a necessity because of legal liability ramifications. For example, if a paraprofessional is supervising some safety aspect of individual practice of a physical education skill, he must be "reasonably prudent," according to law, since he is operating "in loco parentis." Second, that the person is "trained to perform" is a prerequisite to effective performance. Some nonteaching duties, such as locker and shower room supervision, may seem too simple to require training, but problems, some of them quite personal in nature, arise on occasion, and the paraprofessional who is trained to recognize them and to deal professionally with them can contribute to overall quality education.

The advantages of using paraprofessionals are many and obvious. Perhaps the biggest disadvantage is that, unless caution is exercised, the teacher is apt to limit severely his personal exposure to students. No dedicated teacher will allow this to happen, however.

NEW CONCEPTS IN FACILITIES OF PHYSICAL EDUCATION

Modular Construction. Modular or "systems" construction consists of bringing together a number of prefabricated subsystems, sometimes called "pods," which make it possible to erect a school building in a matter of a few months and at a considerable reduction in cost. Reduced cost alone is perhaps sufficient justification for such construction, but one of the greatest advantages is its extreme flexibility. Interior space can be readily rearranged by moving partitions and relocating lighting, ventilation and heating ducts, and other components. Such renovation is in no way so costly as is the remodeling of conventional school buildings.[4]

---

4. Velma Adams, "The Trend to School Building Systems," *School Management* (August 1969), p. 30.

Interior of Idaho State University Minidome, a new concept in all-weather, low-cost sports facility. Photo courtesy of Department of Physical Education, Idaho State University.

Dome-shaped and Air-supported Structures. The number of structures of this type is increasing each year. A dome-shaped building is comparatively less expensive than a traditional one to erect, and it is usually more readily adaptable for multiple use. Spectator facilities must not usurp instructional space. With good planning, a structure that accomodates both can be erected. As for air-supported structures, researchers are working on a system to reinforce an "air only" structure by the use of cable systems which transmit forces to the ground rather than to the enclosure itself and which use inexpensive plastic sheets as membranes rather than coated fabric.[5]

Artificial Surfaces. Artificial surfaces have now been developed for almost all types of physical education instruction. The various synthetic grass surfaces were the first on the market, and many football fields are now covered with such

5. P. R. Theibert, "New Ideas in Physical Education Facilities," *Physical Education Supplement* (Croft Educational Services, 1970), p. 4.

University of Utah sports and special events center, seating capacity 15,000. Photo courtesy of Department of Physical Education, University of Utah.

turf. Although there is not universal agreement on the value of artificial turf, its use to date has fairly well established the fact that it takes a maximum of hard and diverse wear with a minimum of maintenance.

In addition to artificial surfaces on playing fields, new surfaces are beginning to replace traditional wooden floors in gymnasia as well as dirt areas in fieldhouses. There are many different types of surfaces, but basically they are all constructed from some type of plastic. According to the various manufacturers, some of the advantages of these surfaces are: (1) they are more durable than wood, but they require less maintenance; (2) all types of balls bounce true with no dead spots; (3) cleats and spikes cannot harm the surface although they are unnecessary because of its nonslip nature; and (4) there is a sharp reduction in fatigue and in the danger of injury.

Ice Arenas. Facilities for ice skating are becoming ever more popular, and they can be incorporated into an all-purpose building, as discussed above. The newest innovation, perhaps the most adaptable and yet the least expensive, is plastic ice. Experiments are now being conducted, and many traveling ice show companies use plastic ice when true ice is unavailable.

Greater flexibility combined with lower costs is of extreme importance in physical education. Facilities for physical education are specialized and extremely expensive; therefore the best construction plan is one that allows for maximum use at minimum cost. Some of the proposed innovations in gymnasium construction include motorized rolling bleachers that serve as

Facilities for ice skating provide worthwhile leisure time opportunities. Photo courtesy of Kent State University News Service.

movable walls, huge overhead doors on outside walls so that in good weather they can be raised to include the outdoor area in the instructional space, and pivot walls that can serve as storage areas, bulletin boards, projection screens, etc., as well as wall space for such games as handball.[6]

INSTRUCTIONAL MEDIA

It would be remiss in a chapter on current trends not to include discussion of the various educational or instructional media that are prevalent today. The

6. Lamar Kelsey, Fred Kolflat, and Robert Schaefer, "New Generation Gyms," *Nation's Schools,* **84** (December 1969).

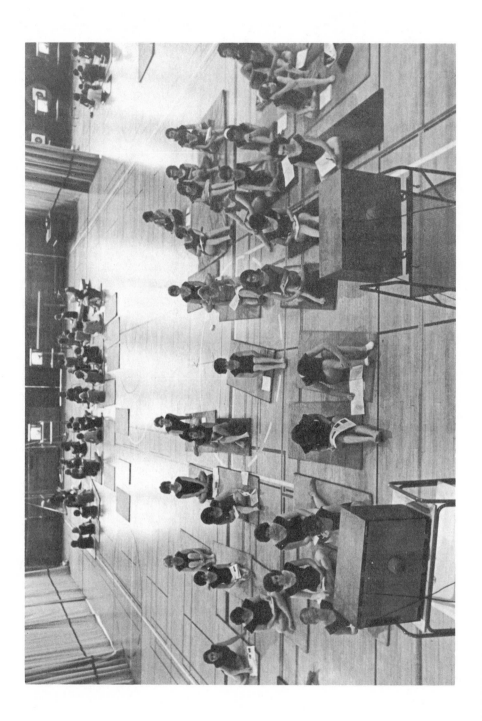

knowledge explosion is but one factor that has fostered the establishment of an instructional media center to replace more traditional audiovisual centers. The increase in the types, numbers, and sophistication of learning aids is also significant. This factor alone dictates central administration of all instructional materials and services for optimum and efficient use. In many schools, the instructional media center is a vital adjunct of the library.

The functions of such a center include the circulation of various kinds of materials, printed and otherwise; production of materials which teachers request, such as slides and filmstrips; and in-service education not only to acquaint teachers with what is available but also to instruct them in the preparation and use of their own materials. In physical education, for example, instant replay television has potential use that is still largely untapped. A very important premise on which effective centers operate is that all resources are readily available to students as well as to teachers. This concept demands space in the center itself where individuals can use the various media available.

Instructional media centers are vital at every level of education, kindergarten through college. Such centers, as well as the media contained within them, naturally become more complex at higher educational levels. It is also obvious that highly competent, trained individuals are needed if the centers are to function properly. Many universities now offer majors or at least minors in instructional media which lead to certification in the area. The demand for teachers educated to design and operate instructional media centers can only increase as many of the other current trends discussed in this chapter become accepted as vital to effective education.

SUMMARY

It is unfortunately true that programs in physical education seem often not to keep pace with changing patterns in education. Why this situation exists is debatable. The reason may be that the school administrator does not conceive of physical education and other "special" subjects as important enough to be considered in overall school change. Or perhaps the physical educator is not creative enough to realize how innovations can be applied effectively in his program. The fact remains that the school program in physical education is *education,* and therefore, even though it has concerns uniquely its own, it must also be cognizant of current educational philosophy and of the innovations which characterize such philosophy. Virtually all philosophers of education

◀Television as an aid to instruction. Photo courtesy of Department of Physical Education for Women, Kent State University.

today subscribe to a theory of educating the whole child, and they contend that such education is a process of using all one's faculties cognitively, effectively, and psycho-motorially.

There is nothing inherently magic in change, nor should proposed innovations be adopted merely to be fashionable. However, it is undeniably true that American schools can stand much improvement, and if some of the current trends seem productive of good, they should be tried and thoroughly evaluated, and on the basis of that evaluation, they should be maintained, altered, or discarded. We cannot overlook the fact that in any commitment to change, the responsibility for proving that one's special educational field is truly educational lies on the shoulders of each individual teacher. And the teacher-coach of physical education has many things going for him that should aid in the educative process. Not the least of them is a shared social involvement between teacher and student in the study of human movement that, if well nurtured, should foster genuine learning.

STUDENT PROJECTS

1. List the advantages and disadvantages of modular scheduling for physical education. If possible, visit a school with each type of scheduling: modular and "traditional." Report on conversation with both students and teachers regarding their evaluation of the type of scheduling they use.

2. If the visits suggested above are impossible, elicit reactions from class members who attended high schools with both types of scheduling.

3. List the advantages and disadvantages of team teaching in physical education. What reasons are given in the literature for the fact that many physical educators seem to shy away from this type of teaching?

4. Visit the instructional media center at your university. Report to the class on the types of services available and the ways in which such services might be implemented at the high school or elementary school level.

5. Survey a sampling of physical education teachers, athletic coaches, and intramural directors in your area to get their reactions to the advantages and disadvantages of artificial surfaces.

6. Start a collection of physical education facility plans including pictures and architects' drawings.

GLOSSARY OF TERMS

Team teaching A program in which two or more teachers cooperatively plan, instruct, and evaluate a class or combination of classes.

Paraprofessionals Mature individuals with training in nonprofessional tasks who are employed to assist the professionals in a particular field.

Differentiated staffing A plan whereby staff members are assigned different levels of responsibility, including teaching, according to their specific abilities.

Modular or flexible scheduling ("mods") Arrangement of the school day into segments of time (modules) which can be combined differently according to the needs of the subject and/or the student.

Modular or systems construction ("pods") The use of prefabricated or precut units in erecting school facilities.

Instructional media center A center where various kinds of teaching and learning aids are housed. These aids range from traditional materials, such as films and slides, to models, printed materials, and instant replay television apparatus.

SELECTED REFERENCES

1. Adams, Velma. "The Trend to School Building Systems." *School Management* (August 1969), pp. 24-30, 49-54.

2. _____. "Why Systems Can't Miss." *School Management* (September 1969), pp. 66-73.

3. Barbee, Don. *Differentiated Staffing: Expectations and Pitfalls.* Washington: National Commission on Teacher Education and Professional Standards, National Education Association, 1969.

4. Christensen, D. Louis. "How 'Mod' Can You Get?" *Ideas Educational,* **6** (Winter 1968), pp. 9-14.

5. English, Fenwick. *Et Tu, Educator, Differentiated Staffing?* Washington: National Commission on Teacher Education and Professional Standards, National Education Association, 1969.

6. Georgiades, William. "Team Teaching: A New Star, Not a Meteor," *Journal of the National Education Association,* **56** (April 1967), pp. 14-15.

7. Kelsey, Lamar, Fred Kolflat, and Robert Schaefer. "New Generation Gyms," *Nation's Schools,* **84** (December 1969), 15 pp. [unnumbered].

8. Mager, Robert F. *Preparing Instructional Objectives.* Palo Alto, Calif: Fearon, 1962.

9. Pearson, Neville P., and Lucius Butler (eds.). *Instructional Materials Centers.* Minneapolis: Burgess, 1969.

10. Pie, Harry E. "What Flexible Scheduling Is All About." *Journal of Health, Physical Education and Recreation* (March 1967), p. 30.

11. Rand, John M., and Fenwick English. "Towards a Differentiated Teaching Staff," *Phi Delta Kappan,* **49** (January 1968), pp. 264-268.

12. Reams, David, and T. J. Bleier. "Developing Team Teaching for Ability Grouping," *Journal of Health, Physical Education and Recreation,* **39** (September 1968).

13. Resick, Matthew C., Beverly L. Seidel, and James Mason. *Modern Administrative Practices in Physical Education and Athletics.* Reading, Mass.: Addison-Wesley, 1970.

14. Ridine, Leonard M. "The Paraprofessional in Physical Education," *The Physical Educator* (October 1970), pp. 114-117.

15. Sadowski, Gregory M. "Flexible Modular Scheduling Allows for Student Choice of Independent Study Units," *Journal of Health, Physical Education and Recreation,* **42** (September 1971), p. 25.

16. Shaplin, Judson T., and Henry F. Olds (eds.). *Team Teaching.* New York: Harper and Row, 1964.

17. Sullivan, Alice and Orlando L. Savastano. "Teacher Aides in Physical

Education," *Journal of Health, Physical Education and Recreation* (May 1969), pp. 26-28.

18. Theibert, P. R. "New Ideas in Physical Education Facilities," in *Physical Education Supplement.* Croft Educational Services, 1970.

19. Trump, J. Lloyd. "Changing School to Serve Individuals Better in HPER." Washington: National Association of Secondary School Principals, unpublished multilithed paper, 1970.

20. _____. "Evaluating Pupil Progress in Team Teaching." Washington: National Association of Secondary School Principals, unpublished multilithed paper, 1970.

21. _____. "How Excellent Are Teaching and Learning in your School?" Washington: National Association of Secondary School Principals, unpublished multilithed paper, 1970.

22. _____. "Presentations and Other Types of Large-Group Instruction," Washington: National Association of Secondary School Principals, unpublished multilithed paper, 1970.

23. Von Bergen, Enid. "Flexible Scheduling for Physical Education," *Journal of Health, Physical Education and Recreation* (March 1967), p. 31.

24. Wiley, W. Deane, and Lloyd K. Bishop. *The Flexibly Scheduled High School.* West Nyack, N.Y.: Parker, 1968.

bio-mechanical foundations

chapter 7

The laws of physics are the decrees of Fate.

ALFRED N. WHITEHEAD

The next three chapters of this text are devoted to the foundations of physical education, as derived from the areas of biomechanics, anatomy, physiology, and the behavioral sciences of sociology and psychology. Physical education is an applied science which finds its basic principles within these scientific areas. Man as a moving, living body obeys the scientific laws of the universe. With adequate knowledge of scientific truths and the application of them to his efforts, man can move more efficiently and propel objects to greater height and distances with accuracy.

For many years the bulk of all research in physical education was centered either in curriculum or in teaching and coaching methods. To fill the need for additional knowledge about the effects of exercise or activity on the human body, the area of exercise physiology developed with its own laboratories and research personnel. Similarly, when more knowledge was needed on how the body moved, both kinesiological and myographic laboratories came into being. More recently, investigation by the profession in the area of motor learning has encompassed both the sociological and the psychological impact of physical activity on man. Research and research facilities in this area are now an integral part of many departments, and the results are being presented in the research sections of many professional meetings.

In this chapter the authors reviewed those laws of physics which have special meaning to man or the materials he uses in his physical activities. Examples from exercise and sports illustrate how adherence to the physical laws can help in both participation and teaching.

Basically, the material is set forth by means of guiding principles for the professional physical educator. A definition of the term "principle" should clarify its use in this context. As used in the field, *principles of physical education are guides to behavior based on truth as determined by the scientific and philosophical knowledge of the times.* When science discovers new truths and philosophic concepts change, or when new philosophies evolve, the underlying principles of the discipline also change.

BIOMECHANICAL SCIENCES—GENERAL COMMENTS

All objects on earth are responsive to the laws of the physical world, whether they are in motion or at complete rest. These laws apply to the body, its movements, and the objects it manipulates. Since all physical activity revolves around human movement, a serious student should understand the internal and external forces which are constantly brought into play. The science of movement stems from the disciplines of biology and physics.

Many physical activities are concerned with the propulsion of objects by lifting, throwing, pushing, or striking. Although most participants operate on the level of kinesthesis (the way the activity feels), the physical education teacher and coach should have a working knowledge of the biomechanical principles involved. He is then able to relate the principles to the various activities and to evaluate instruction and performance in the light of his knowledge. He may violate one of the principles to achieve a greater adherence to another. For example, he might sacrifice stability to increase forward movement, knowing the price he must pay for that decision.

Entire textbooks have been written about the physical and mechanical principles as they apply to a single sports activity. Therefore the examples of physical principles chosen here are such that they apply to most sports, with specific reference to selected ones for purposes of clarification and explanation. The mechanics of physical activity is a relatively new and fertile field for study and research.

INTERNAL FORCES OF HUMAN MOVEMENT

The body moves and applies force to objects by contracting muscles, which act across joints by means of a system of levers. When a stimulus reaches a muscle through a motor nerve impulse, biological energy is converted to mechanical movement. The intensity of the movement depends on the number of muscle fibers stimulated.

The levers in the body follow the classification used in the external physical world. The classifications are made according to the location of the axis (fulcrum) in relation to the two forces, effort and resistance. In a first-class lever, the fulcrum (A) is located between the resistance (R) and the effort (E), as illustrated in Fig. 7.1. Common examples of this type of lever are crowbars, scissors, pliers, balances (scales), and seesaws. The extension of the arm at the elbow by the triceps and the extension of the foot at the ankle when not bearing weight are examples within the body. In terms of work done by any effort, this type of lever is the most efficient.

In the second-class lever, the resistance, or weight, is located between the

Figure 7.1

Figure 7.2

fulcrum and the effort, or force (Fig. 7.2). Examples of this type are a wheelbarrow, a nutcracker, and a paper trimmer. One of the very few examples of this type of lever in the body is the lower jaw.

Most levers of the human body are of the third class, in which the effort is located between the fulcrum and the resistance (Fig. 7.3). Shovels, sugar tongs, and grass shears are examples of third-class levers. Two examples in the human body are the flexions of the lower arm and lower leg. This lever lends itself to the development of speed of movement, because the resistance arm is longer than the force arm.

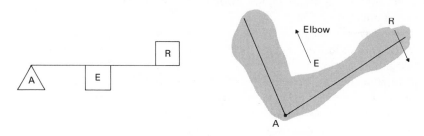

Figure 7.3

In all three lever types, a state of balance or equilibrium is determined by the formula,

Force × Force arm = Resistance × Resistance arm.

Movement results from an increase in either force or resistance or from the shortening or lengthening of either of the two arms. In the first-class lever, a great resistance can be overcome with little force by lengthening the force arm. In the human body, one may obtain speed of movement by using a force on a resistance with a long resistance arm. Implements such as rackets, paddles, oars, and bats increase the length of the lever arms.

In most movements of the body, a number of levers come into action simultaneously or in sequence. This fact may require the stabilizing of other parts of the body, as occurs in heavy weight lifting.

CENTER OF GRAVITY

For a definition of gravity or gravitation, Sir Isaac Newton's principle should suffice. He stated that between any two objects in the world there exists a mutual force of attraction that is directly proportional to the product of the masses of the objects and inversely proportional to the square of their distances apart. Since the earth has such an enormous mass, the attraction to it is greater than between two smaller objects. For example, if one held two baseballs at arm's length and released them, the attraction between them would be negligible in comparison with the attraction of each to the mass of the earth (Fig. 7.4). The baseballs would fall to earth; thus the weight of an object is determined by this gravitational pull of the earth. An object is attracted to earth with the acceleration of 32 feet per second for each second of fall (wind resistance discounted).

Figure 7.4

In all physical activities these principles apply. Objects propelled in sports are affected in their flight, as is the body when it swings, hangs, and moves. The center of gravity of a body is the point at which its whole weight can be brought into balance. In a simple symmetrical object like a ball, the center of gravity is usually the literal center. In an irregularly shaped object like the human body or a baseball bat, it may be more difficult to determine. The human body moves and its parts change their relationships to one another; with such changes there is a change in the center of gravity. For example, the raising of the arms over the head elevates the center of gravity by several centimeters.

In both equilibrium and motion, the center of gravity plays an important role. The stable position of the defensive football lineman or of the wrestler differs from that of a trackman on the starting blocks. The body is balanced when the center of gravity is above the base of support. That result can be achieved by simply spreading the feet apart, but if one carries the adjustment to extremes, he becomes so stable he cannot move. The larger base gives a greater balance in that the center of gravity is kept within the base. The center of gravity in the human body may vary from person to person according to body build and sex. The center of gravity of the male is usually higher than that of the female. Movements during walking, running, and kicking will raise, lower, or change the lateral position of the center of gravity.

In running events the center of gravity is kept in front of the base of support to give a pulling effect. In tumbling and diving a high center of gravity helps the performer in rotary movements. The offensive backs in football use a stance that is different from that of the defensive lineman. The degree of stability necessary for these positions varies; hence the center of gravity of the players is altered.

MOTION

It is only fitting to begin a study of physical principles of motion with a discussion of Newton's three laws of motion. In 1687 Sir Isaac Newton wrote a treatise on motion which became the basis of modern mechanics. Newton propounded three simple basic laws of motion, which are equally applicable today with a few minor exceptions that are far beyond the scope of this text.

Newton's first law: Every body (object) persists in a state of rest or of uniform motion in a straight line unless compelled by external forces to change that state.

This law of motion deals with the overcoming of the tendency of rest or, in physical terms, overcoming inertia. Let us examine some examples from activity. In track or baseball the runner makes better time from a running start than from a stationary one. The baseball runner must tag up (touch base) before advancing on a fly ball. He would be at an advantage approaching the base from the far side and timing his touch with the catch. Some years ago a rule was placed in the books to prohibit this approach. A quarter miler achieves better time from a flying start, as in a relay, than he does from a dead start. Other examples of this principle are the windup of the pitcher (he starts moving the baseball) or the push-off in bowling, which puts the ball in motion to overcome the inertia of twelve to sixteen pounds at rest and results in a greater ball speed and smoother delivery.

An illustration of persistence in motion in a straight line is the tendency of the base runner or trackman to swing wide in making his turns; he must apply force to the base, ground, or track to change this tendency. A base runner slides into the base to avoid overrunning it, since his body persists in a state of motion. The hammer thrower has to pull inward to prevent the hammer from flying off in a tangent.

Hammer thrower pulls inward to keep hammer from flying off in a straight line. Photo courtesy of Kent State University Athletic Department.

Newton's second law: When a body (object) is acted upon by a force, its resultant acceleration (change of speed) is proportional to the force and inversely proportional to the mass.

One of the forces which must be contended with in activity is gravity. This constant force of 32 feet per second/per second must be considered in such events as the high jump, and pole vault and in throwing events. The golfer must

consider the force necessary to propel the ball to the green by changing his club or the speed of his swing. The basketball player must learn the force necessary to reach the basket from different ranges within the shooting area.

Newton's third law: For every force or action there is an equal and opposite reaction.

In physical activity and sports, this particular law of motion plays a major role. The act of moving one's body on air, land, and water depends on it. When a sprinter pushes against the surface of the track, the reaction propels him forward. When the swimmer presses against the water, the reaction propels him in the opposite direction. The force exerted on the floor elevates the body in a push-up. Finally, in all striking activities, action and reaction occur. When two such objects as a racket and a ball meet, there is a reaction in both. This phenomenon will be explored more fully in the next few sections.

CONSERVATION OF MOMENTUM

In a collision between two objects, whatever momentum is gained by one object has been lost by the other, and the momentum of the whole system remains the same. This principle may be shown by the formula

$$MV + M'V' = MU + M'U',$$

where M represents the mass of the first object, and V its velocity before the collision, M' and V' respectively the weight and velocity of the second object. After the collison, U and U' represent the new velocities of the first and second objects, respectively. In a specific example, a pitched baseball with a mass of 5 oz is traveling at 90 mph and strikes a 32 oz bat traveling at 90 mph. If the speed of the bat is reduced to 80 mph, the hit ball will travel at 154 mph. Transferring these values to the formula above, we have

$$(5)(90) + 32(90) = (5)(x) + 32(80),$$

and solving for x gives us the speed of 154 mph for the hit ball.

The swing speed of the striking end of the bat is the most important factor. Within limits, a lighter bat permits the average player to develop this speed without a significant loss in the total sum of forces. The batter's stride, pivot, and wrist action all contribute to the speed of the striking portion of the bat. In a similar problem, a golf ball sitting on a tee is struck by a driver. The entire sum

◀For every action there is an equal and opposite reaction. Photo courtesy of Kent State University Athletic Department.

of the momentum gained by both driver and ball must be supplied by the driver, since the golf ball is at rest at the start, and therefore the mass of the golf ball is multiplied by zero velocity. As in the baseball example, the club head speed is the dominating factor if we assume that all the other conditions remain stable. The same principle holds true for a ball dropped on a hard-surface floor of an infinite mass. Theoretically, the ball will rebound to the height from which it falls. However, the formula above requires the following conditions: (1) the objects meet at the center of gravity

or, as expressed in sports, "on the button"; (2) the objects travel without rotation or spin; (3) there is no heat or sound energy lost; and (4) the objects have a perfect "coefficient of restitution," or elasticity. The loss of speed is explained by these four factors since the principle of conservation of energy holds that *energy cannot be manufactured or destroyed; it can only be directed in its flow or transformed.*

COEFFICIENT OF RESTITUTION

One of the conditions cited for the perfect conservation of momentum was that of a perfect "coefficient of restitution." This term simply means that the object can return to its original shape rapidly after being compressed by a blow. This capability varies in accordance with differences in materials and methods used in the construction of the objects. Golf balls especially vary in this quality. Cheaper balls are usually less elastic, in addition to having other undesirable features, such as low resistance to cuts and less whiteness of cover. A ball filled with air is easily compressed, but it returns to its original shape more slowly than does a solid ball of elastic material. A simple test can demonstrate this principle. With a yardstick held perpendicular to a hard, smooth surface, have several balls dropped a distance of one yard to the surface, and record the heights of the rebounds. For each ball the percentage of return, which shows the amount of elasticity, is its "coefficient of restitution." The readings could vary from 0 to a perfect coefficient of 1 (Fig. 7.5).

For obtaining an exact coefficient of restitution, we have the formula[1]

$$e = \frac{hb}{hd},$$

1. John W. Bunn, *Scientific Principles of Coaching* (New York: Prentice-Hall, 1955), pp. 65-66.

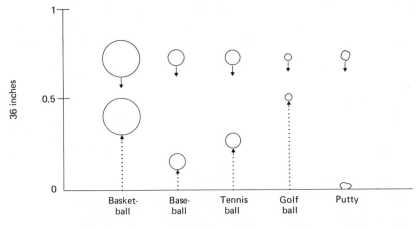

Figure 7.5

where *e* is the coefficient of elasticity, *hb* is the height of the bounce, and *hd* is the height of the drop.

The elastic quality of a ball may be altered by a change in temperature. Handballs are often placed in hot water prior to use to make them livelier. In recent years a number of baseball managers have been accused of keeping baseballs under refrigeration when playing teams of superior hitting abilities. Some differences can be expected in balls of the same materials and workmanship, and such differences tend to be more noticeable when there is a loss of elasticity due to use and aging.

ROTATION OR SPIN

Much of the success of a participant in games involving balls (especially round ones) is due to his ability to impart the proper amount of rotation or spin in the direction desired. The baseball pitcher, the golfer, the handball player, the tennis player, and the bowler have much in common in that the rotation of the manipulated object may be the key to success. A "moving" fastball or one that leaves its initial line of flight is harder to hit than is one that travels faster but straighter.

What are the physical laws of rotation and spin, and how do they function? A simplified explanation is that when a struck or thrown ball is spinning, the side that turns into the air wall (or solid material) meets with increased resistance, whereas the side turning away from the direction of flight meets less resistance and therefore tends to accelerate. This combination of circumstances causes the ball to rise, fall, hook, or slice. When a backspin is imparted to it, a ball will tend to rise and, on striking a surface, to turn toward the striker or thrower. This explains both the "hop" (rise) on a fastball in baseball, and the backspin on a golf ball that is properly hit to the green (Fig. 7.6). The ball

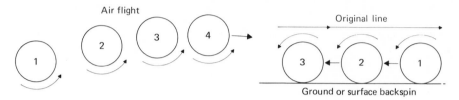

Figure 7.6

follows the path of least resistance, as shown in Fig. 7.7. The ball is impeded in its turn in toward the surface at point A but free to turn at point B.

Figure 7.7

If top spin is imparted to it, a ball will drop faster, because of the factors described above, but it will roll away from the thrower or striker (Fig. 7.8). The rebound will be harder and faster. Tennis and table tennis players use top spin to cause the ball to strike in a prescribed area and rebound rapidly. In baseball the "sinker" or "drop" ball pitcher uses this technique.

Figure 7.8

A clockwise rotation imparted to a ball will cause the ball to move toward the thrower's or striker's right (Fig. 7.9). If he is right-handed, he makes his

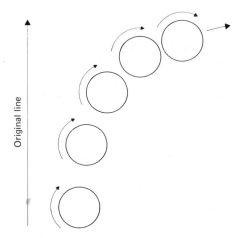

Figure 7.9

bowling ball fade, he slices in golf, and he throws an in-curve in baseball. In striking games there is usually some loss of distance because of clockwise rotation.

A counterclockwise rotation imparted to a ball by a right-handed striker or thrower moves the ball to the left of the original line of flight (Fig. 7.10). This results in an out-curve for the pitcher and a hook for the bowler or golfer.

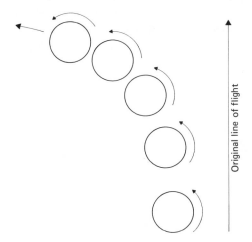

Figure 7.10

Other objects in sports have special problems. When a football is kicked (punted) or thrown, it is rotated in order to stabilize it and to reduce the wind resistance. The nose is elevated or depressed, depending on the distance desired or the wind conditions. The discus and the javelin have special problems of aerodynamics because of their size and shape. These problems and others are studied in advanced courses in the mechanics of physical activities.

SUMMARY

Teachers and coaches must have an understanding of simple mechanics since the human body moves within the framework of these universal laws. Furthermore, the implements used in sports can be handled more efficiently if both player and coach have an understanding of the basic principles involved. Although scientific principles are sometimes defied with some degree of success, the instructor should have an understanding of what is lost or gained by such defiance.

When a baseball player, golfer, or tennis player selects a longer bat, club, or racquet or a heavier one, he should be aware of the consequences of his choice. If a player has a choice between a stiff shaft and a flexible one, the teacher should point out the advantages and disadvantages of each. It is not enough for the teacher or coach to instruct student players in how to perform; he must also explain why they should perform in that way.

Finally, bodily injuries may occur when mechanical principles are ignored or insufficiently understood. The acts of standing and walking, if done improperly, may result in weak and fallen arches. Improper lifting may cause a painful back condition. Throwing curve balls (especially the screwball) may cause permanent damage to young baseball players who are allowed to throw an excessive number of them.

STUDENT PROJECTS

1. Bring to class various balls that are normally used in different sports. Impart spin to them on the floor and on the desk tops. Observe the path taken by a ball after it strikes an obstruction, such as a wall.

2. Drop a number of balls of different types from the same level and observe the height of the rebound. Estimate the coefficients of restitution.

GLOSSARY OF TERMS

Principles Guides to behavior based on truth as determined by the scientific and philosophical knowledge of the times.

Kinesiology The study of human motion.

Center of gravity The point at which the whole weight of a body can be brought into balance.

Conservation of momentum The principle that total momentum remains the same in a collision between two objects. Whatever momentum is gained by one object has been lost by the other.

Coefficient of restitution The rate at which an object returns to its original shape after being compressed by a blow.

SELECTED REFERENCES

1. Broer, Marian R. *Efficiency of Human Movement.* Philadelphia: W. B. Saunders, 1960.

2. Bunn, John W. *Scientific Principles of Coaching.* New York: Prentice-Hall, 1955.

3. Constant, F. Woodbridge. *Fundamental Principles of Physics.* Reading, Mass.: Addison-Wesley, 1967.

4. Dyson, Geoffrey H. G. *The Mechanics of Athletics,* 4th ed. London: University of London Press, 1967.

5. Read, Albert J. *Physics: A Descriptive Analysis.* Reading, Mass.: Addison-Wesley, 1970.

6. Scott, M. Gladys. *Analysis of Human Motion.* New York: Appleton-Century-Crofts, 1963.

7. Trickner, R. A. R., and B. J. K. Trickner. *The Science of Movement.* New York: American Elsevier, 1967.

8. Wickstrom, Ralph L. *Fundamental Motor Patterns.* Philadelphia: Lea and Febiger, 1970, pp. 16-19.

9. Williams, Marian, and Herbert R. Lessner. *Biomechanics of Human Motion.* Philadelphia: W. B. Saunders, 1962, pp. 111-128.

anatomical and physiological foundations

chapter 8

Health is the vital principle of bliss,
And exercise, of health.

JAMES THOMSON

How the body is structured (anatomy) and how it functions (physiology) determine to a great degree how a person performs physical activities, including athletic sports. Some capacities of a given individual are established at conception by the genetic characteristics inherited from parents. Others can be changed by conditioning the systems of the body to perform the desired activities at optimum levels. The purpose of this chapter is to examine some general anatomical and physiological principles and the practical application of these principles in specific situations. Study in depth in these areas is essential for all teachers of physical education, who will find the opportunity for such study in most curricula of teacher preparation institutions offering a major program.

ANATOMICAL PRINCIPLES

The body type (build) of an individual has an important influence on physical performance.

There are a number of ways of determining body types (somatotyping), from that of Sheldon, who classified three basic body types, to that of Wetzel, who devised nine channels. There are very few pure body types. Most individuals have characteristics from two of Sheldon's types, occasionally with a few from the third. The three principal body types as described by Sheldon follow.

Endomorphic. A person with endomorphic characteristics is usually short, soft in appearance, and rounded in contour. His head is large and rounded, his neck is short and thick, his shoulders are rounded, his chest is barrel-shaped, and his abdomen larger than his chest. His arms and legs are short and thick, and he has short, pudgy fingers and toes.

Mesomorphic. A person with mesomorphic characteristics is muscular, of medium height, and square or triangular in appearance. His head is average with square features, his neck is average in length but muscular, and his shoulders are wide and square. His chest is broad and elliptical, his buttocks and hips are small, his arms and legs are average in length but muscular in outline, and his hands and feet are average in size.

Ectomorphic. A person with ectomorphic characteristics is usually tall, thin, and sharp-featured. His head is small, his features sharp, and he has a long, thin neck. His shoulders are narrow and thin, his chest is narrow, and he has a long trunk. His arms and legs are long and thin, and his hands and feet are large.

The average female, in comparison with the average male, tends toward the endomorphic type. Several subprinciples involving this comparison follow.

Examples of different body types. Photo courtesy of Department of Physical Education for Women, Kent State University.

1. The carrying angle (arm angle) is greater in the female than in the male. As illustrated in Fig. 8.1, the narrowness of the shoulders of the female and the width of the pelvic girdle contribute to this difference, which expresses itself in the fact that girls carry books at the breast level, whereas boys carry them at the extended arm position. Another example of the effect of the carrying angle is suggested by the off-center placement of the handle in modern luggage in order to give a better mechanical advantage. Note, however, that the difference in carrying angle is not the principal reason that girls throw differently than boys; the reason is more likely to be that they were not given proper instruction during their formative years.

2. The oblique leg line is greater in the female than the male. The female's broader pelvic girdle after adolescence gives her femur a marked obliquity compared with that of the male. As the schematic view of Fig. 8.2 indicates, the mechanical advantage remains with the male. The greater obliquity produces side

Female   Male

Figure 8.1

sway and oscillation; the latter in turn reduces forward speed and resembles the side sway produced by cross-body arm action in running. Fashion models exaggerate this movement when they walk by placing one foot before the other.

This principle is illustrated by the excellent girl runners who tend to have the body build depicted in the diagram on the right. They have very little side sway and therefore greater forward speed.

Female   Male

Figure 8.2

3. The pelvis of the female is wider and more shallow than that of the male.
Although the wider pelvis of the female is important for childbearing, the greater

prominence of the hips works to her disadvantage in the preceding two subprinciples. Female pelvises are not all of the same shape, however, and some women have the narrow, deep pelvis of the male, which may complicate the delivery of their children. In all areas of bodily differences specified in these three subprinciples, there may be variations. The female may have the structure described as male, whereas some males have wide hips, narrow shoulders, and lower centers of gravity, all of which are normally associated with the female. Such males may lose the mechanical advantage of forward running speed but gain in increased balance. The schematic view shown in Fig. 8.3, which combines Figs. 8.1 and 8.2, suggests the reason for the female's lower center of gravity as compared with that of the male. The advantages of both high and low centers of gravity were discussed in Chapter 7. In summary, it may be stated that the two extremes in body types have often been maligned by the physical educator or coach; when he stresses getting in "shape," he means the shape of the ideal mesomorph. However, the body type of an individual sets limits on the changes that can be made in the body by diet or activity. No amount of exercise

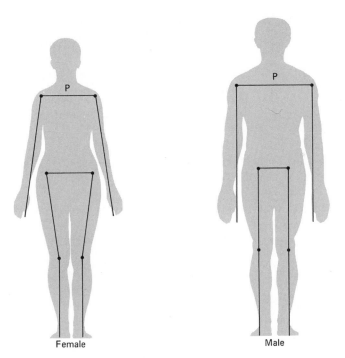

Female   Male

Figure 8.3. A composite schematic view of the typical male and female figures, depicting the differences in arm angle, shoulder width, and pelvic width, as well as the obliquity of the femur.

would change a St. Bernard into a terrier, and no endomorph will change into an ectomorph. However, he may become a slimmer endomorph.

The endomorphic body types are often found among the football tackles and guards and in the weight events in track and field. Ectomorphs often dominate the long-distance running events, and they usually fill the center and forward positions in basketball. A low center of gravity is advantageous to a football fullback, whereas a high center of gravity helps a sprinter, because it is thrust forward, thus creating a pulling effect. Clearly there are advantages and disadvantages in all body types.

PHYSIOLOGICAL PRINCIPLES

The environmental temperature has an effect on physical performance.

When the environmental temperature rises above 80° F, body metabolism also rises. The number of respirations per minute increases by five or six with each rise of 1.8°F in rectal temperature. There is a rapid increase in pulse rate. There is a decrement in working capacity at 90°F from that at 70° F. In essence, extreme heat has the effect of detraining on an individual.

The human body can become acclimatized to heat. The period from the first exposure to the point at which acclimatization is well developed averages from five to eight days. The adjustment is less difficult if there is good physical conditioning, but it can be retarded by low salt and water intakes. Both water and salt should be available to the participant, but they should be used with care. For example, acclimatization is not improved by a higher than adequate salt intake. Acclimatization to heat is partially retained for several weeks and with occasional exposure can be extended for months.

The application of this principle is important in early football seasons, when heat stress tends to be a threat. Some states have forbidden the use of protective equipment for the first few days of practice for high school football players because it retards heat loss. At the college level, individual conferences have invoked a similar rule. Teams going to a hot climate to play (bowl games, for example) often arrive a week or two in advance of games in order to become acclimatized.

A cold environment also affects performance. Players do not receive enough benefits from warm-up. Furthermore, players on the bench and fans in the bleachers tighten their muscles in a cold environment. After a long period, these muscles are as fatigued as they would be if they had been used. The act of shivering is also fatiguing.

Water ingestion does not impede physical performance.

As a result of heat stress studies, there has been a decided reversal in the use of water during periods of vigorous physical performance. Whereas it was once common practice to forbid the use of water even in heat stress, water (or other liquids) is now made readily available, and participants are urged to replace lost fluids.

Since water makes up about seventy-five percent of muscle mass and salt another five percent, and since the composition of blood is eighty percent water, losses during heavy exercise on hot, humid days may be as great as five or six percent of body weight. Replacement of water without salt replacement may still result in dehydration, since one of the functions of salt is to hold water in suspension in the cells.

In laboratory studies, ingestion of up to a liter did not interfere with performance. For some athletes, the ingestion of larger amounts of water seemed to make them lazy, and the incentive or motive for good performance was then missing. Liquids other than water (isotonic liquids) have been marketed for their property of being assimilated more rapidly than water. Additional objective evidence of the advantages of this medium is still needed.

Altitude has an effect on physical performance.

Anyone who read about, took part in, or watched the 1968 Olympics in Mexico City became aware of the effects of high altitude on performance. Whether the effects were physiological or psychological was at times hard to discern. One year in advance of the Olympics, seventy doctors from a number of participating countries were supposedly studying the effects of altitude in Mexico City.

Lung ventilation increases progressively with increases in altitude. The reduction in the partial pressure of oxygen necessitates breathing more air in the attempt to obtain the same amount of oxygen as at sea level. The amount of oxygen necessary for a given physical activity remains the same at all altitudes. However, the increased work of the muscles of respiration requires the consumption of additional oxygen. At altitudes of about 7000 feet, respiration may increase as much as one-third.

Without sufficient oxygen, heart rates for work increase and blood pressure rises. Short bursts of work are not affected if they are not dependent on oxygen uptake. This fact was well summarized by deVries:

> Not all athletic performances suffer because of the hypoxia of higher altitudes. Obviously "one maximal effort" activities such as shot put, long jump, high jump, etc., do not suffer because they do not depend upon O_2 transport. Furthermore, events of less than one minute duration, such as the

A six-channel physiograph during a physical work capacity test. Photo courtesy of Exercise Physiology Laboratory, Kent State University.

100 and 200 yard dashes, are also performed (very largely) anaerobically, and consequently they are unimpaired (but recovery times are longer).[1]

1. Herbert A. deVries, *Physiology of Exercise for Physical Education and Athletics* (Dubuque, Iowa: Wm. C. Brown, 1966), pp. 277-278.

Measurement of oxygen uptake during treadmill running, with electrocardiograph monitoring. Photo courtesy of Exercise Physiology Laboratory, Kent State University.

The human body has a remarkable ability to acclimatize to altitude as well as to heat. Although some individuals do not acclimatize readily, most begin to do so in about a week, and adjustment increases with additional time spent. This acclimatization lasts to some degree for a period of about one month after return to a lower altitude. Balke lists the factors in acclimatization to altitude changes.

These mechanisms are: increased pulmonary ventilation with accompanying changes of the acid-base balance of the blood, improved diffusing capacity for oxygen in the lungs as manifested by a decrease in the alveolar-arterial (A-a) gradient for oxygen, and the increase of the red blood cell count as well as the hemoglobin content of the blood.[2]

2. Harold B. Falls (ed.), *Exercise Physiology* (New York: Academic Press, 1968), p. 249.

The physically fit individual has a greater aerobic capacity than the unfit individual.

Aerobic work is a result of that process by which chemical energy is converted into muscular work with the utilization of oxygen and without the development of an oxygen debt. Several factors benefit the physically fit individual: (a) his heart is larger because of his training; (b) his resting pulse rate is lower; (c) his stroke volume (volume of blood expelled from the heart with each beat) is greater; (d) his capillary bed (number of capillaries per cubic centimeter of muscle tissue) is greater; and (e) the using muscle cell of the individual is able to utilize the available oxygen to a greater degree.

The reciprocal innervation of pairs of antagonistic muscles results in smooth and harmonious movement.

According to deVries,

In the case of the flexion reflex—in order that it might proceed with dispatch—the antagonistic extensor muscle group must be prevented from acting. This inhibition of the antagonists is accomplished by kinesthetic impulses from the muscle spindles of the flexor muscle and these synapse not only with the flexor motor neuron directly, but also, indirectly, with the motor neurons of extensor muscles of the same joint.[3]

Most athletic sports demand this type of smooth action. Hitting a golf ball or baseball, catching, shooting a basketball, and diving are examples. One needs only to go to an ice or roller skating arena to observe the defiance of this principle in action. The tightening of both sets of antagonistic muscles results in jerky and uncoordinated movement.

Outside stimuli, such as fear, pressure, cold, and criticism, can bring about undesirable results. For example, a beginner may hit a golf ball well, and yet, when faced with an obstacle such as a pond in front of the tee, he may ignore the principle underlying the relaxing of antagonistic muscles.

Teaching and coaching, which emphasize relaxation, contribute to smoother performance of activities. Opportunities to play under less stressful situations and under game conditions can contribute to a relaxed performance.

At one time it was believed that heavy weight-lifting was detrimental to anyone who wished to perform in activities that demand smooth action. There has been no evidence to substantiate this belief.

Muscle tissue increases in size (hypertrophy) with increased use (work) and decreases in size (atrophy) with disuse.

---

3. deVries, *op. cit.*, p. 34.

Electromyographic recording during test of isometric strength test. Photo courtesy of Electromyographic Laboratory, Kent State University.

Normally called the overload principle of work, this principle is important in that there is a high correlation between increase in muscle size and increase in muscle strength, although there can in fact be an increase in strength without an increase in size. Increase in muscle size is due to an increase not in the number but in the size of the fibers and the intramuscular tissue.

A muscle can be overloaded in either of two ways. When overloaded isotonically, the muscle shortens; when overloaded isometrically, the muscle remains the same in length. Advocates of both systems of exercise can be found. The muscles can be exercised isometrically by exertion, without equipment, against such immovable objects as walls and floors. The original investigators, Hettinger and Mueller, indicated that a maximum effect could be obtained by one six-second isometric contraction against two-thirds of an individual's maximum effort. Subsequent investigators have modified the number of seconds and the intensity of the effort. There are two important weaknesses of this system of muscle development: there is very little cardiovascular development, and the strength development may be restricted mainly to that one angle in the whole range of motion in a joint.

Isotonic exercise depends on the use of resistive exercise of submaximum effort with four to eight repetitions. The motivational factor is greater in isotonic exercises because the individual can see the changes more readily—that is, they can be more easily measured. A greater number of repetitions enhances the improvement of muscular endurance.

Physical conditioning brings about beneficial physiological changes.

In addition to the changes already noted, vigorous physical exercise enhances the functioning of the body in a number of ways. Some are discussed in the following paragraphs.

Measurement of cardiac output by the carbon dioxide rebreathing method. Photo courtesy of Exercise Physiology, Kent State University.

1. The resting heart rate of a conditioned individual becomes slower and more efficient. This change occurs in the overall-conditioned athlete rather than in one conditioned to perform a single activity, such as lifting. The heart as an organ is probably efficient up to about 180 beats per minute. The conditioned individual is able to perform many more difficult physical activities before his heart reaches that level than can an individual whose heart beat is 20 to 30 beats higher per minute while at rest. Although the average heart rate is approximately 76 to 78 beats per minute, the highly conditioned athlete may have a rate in the 40's.

2. The heart size of a conditioned individual increases with activity. Since the heart is made up of muscle tissue, the trained individual's heart, in addition to having better tonus, is expected to increase somewhat in size. Note, however, that this increase in size (hypertrophy) should not be confused with distension of the heart, which is pathological in nature.

3. The conditioned individual has a larger heart stroke volume than an unconditioned one. Stroke volume, the amount of blood ejected from the heart with each beat, increases slightly during exercise. A greater stroke volume, combined with an increase in heart rate, results in the greater cardiac output necessary for the transportation of oxygen that will affect the delay of fatigue.

4. The conditioned athlete's total volume of blood and the amount of his hemoglobin exceed those of the unconditioned individual. The volume may increase by as much as ten percent. Since the stroke volume partially depends on the blood volume available, this increase is beneficial in prevention and recovery from fatigue.

Common drugs may have an effect on physical performance.

Since common drugs have varied physiological effects, we will examine them individually in terms of their benefits or deleterious effects. We will not deal here with illegal drugs, since their illegality should preclude their use.

1. Nicotine (as found in tobacco) has been the theme of many discussions and a basis of extensive research. The evidence that links smoking to lung cancer should be the overriding consideration in all of these discussions. Although it is a stimulant, nicotine depresses the production of adrenalin and constricts the blood vessels (the smaller ones drastically). This factor has had a long-standing association with heart disease. A long period of smoking causes a pulmonary fibrosis (thickening of cells of the pulmonary tract). Smoking also causes an inhalation of carbon monoxide, which interferes with oxygen uptake. Although the effects of nicotine are temporary in nature, sufficient time should elapse to allow for its removal from the body before competition is attempted. There is no evidence whatsoever of benefits to justify its use.

2. Alcohol is a transitory stimulant and then becomes a depressant. It is also a vasodilator. Its first depressant effects are noticed in the judgment centers (frontal lobe) rather than in the motor centers of the brain. Stories of athletes who drank and still achieved greatness have been used as an argument for permissiveness with some athletes. The problem is complicated in certain communities, where ethnic groups use both wine and beer as part of their staple diet. However, evidence does not warrant the use of a drug that can impair judgment.

3. Amphetamine sulfate is a stimulant to the nervous system. It raises the blood pressure and heart rate, and it retards the recovery of both. Golding and Barnard[4] found that d-amphetamine sulfate had no significant effects on the performance of conditioned or unconditioned subjects in either the rested or the fatigued state. Most other research has produced similar results. Evidence does not warrant use to enhance performance; such use may, in fact, interfere with the rest necessary to good performance.

4. Caffeine, an ingredient of both coffee and tea, is a vasoconstrictor and yet has a dilative effect on the coronary artery. It stimulates the central nervous system and does delay the onset of fatigue. There is some evidence that it may cause impairment in coordination (Graf), that larger than normal amounts of lactic acid appear from muscles exposed to caffeine, and that muscle metabolism (O_2 consumption) is elevated when it is present (Hartree and Hill.) As a diuretic, caffeine stimulates the kidneys and may increase production by several hundred percent. Since coffee and tea are consumed extensively in our culture, their use is almost impossible to control. Still, it need not be advocated.

5. Anabolic steroids are widely used by weight lifters, weight men in track, and football players. These commercial steroids have the same effects as does testosterone, which is produced in the normal male. There is some evidence that steroids have an effect on muscle strength and body weight when they are used in combination with an adequate protein diet and a program of weight training. The extent of these changes is now undergoing study. Unfortunately, there are several known and suspected side effects that raise serious doubts as to the wisdom of such use. Among them are the impairment of liver function, premature cessation of long-bone growth in the prepubertal boy, change in size of testes, suppression of pituitary action, and acute muscular cramping during activity. Until more definite long-range findings are available, the use of anabolic steroids is hazardous at best.

4. L. A. Golding and R. J. Barnard, "The Effect of d-Amphetamine Sulfate on Physical Performance," *Journal of Sports Medicine and Physical Fitness,* 3 (December 1963), pp. 221-224.

There are a number of physiological and anatomical differences between the adult male and female which have a bearing on physical activity.

The differences that may affect fatigue and recovery include the following.

1. The number of red blood cells (erythrocytes) per cubic millimeter is greater for male than for female. The male has approximately 5 million red blood cells, the female 4½ million.
2. The average male heart is larger than the average female heart.
3. The average heart rate of the male is lower than that of the female.
4. The average male has more hemoglobin per 100 millimeters of blood than does the average female.
5. The basal metabolic rate is higher for the male than for the female.
6. The cardiac cost of a workload is less for a male than for a female.
7. At a given workload, the oxygen uptake of the female is lower than that of the male.

The statements above reinforce the knowledge that the male has greater capacity to resist fatigue and recovers more rapidly from fatigue than the female.

SUMMARY

The purpose of presenting a selected number of anatomical and physiological principles is to provide knowledge about the body and its functions that is essential for a good teacher of physical education. Such knowledge sets him apart from the technician, who may know how to do something without knowing the reasons for doing it. The knowledgeable physical educator can explain why exercise is good and how performance is enhanced when it is based on scientific principles. This background is the basis of good instruction.

STUDENT PROJECTS

1. Observe different athletic teams and record the positions filled by players with different body types.
2. If the department has a physiology of exercise laboratory, visit it and observe the types of activities under research.

GLOSSARY OF TERMS

Somatotyping Determination of body types by matching with a series of predetermined characteristics.

Aerobic Pertaining to work done by muscle with the utilization of oxygen.

Anaerobic Pertaining to work done by muscle without the utilization of oxygen and resulting in an oxygen debt.

Atrophy Reduction in muscle size due to lack of activity.

Hypertrophy Increase in muscle size due to activity.

Isotonic Pertaining to exercise that includes movement with resistance and a shortening of muscles.

Isometric Pertaining to exercise that includes resistance but no movement or change in muscle length.

SELECTED REFERENCES

1. Basmajian, J. V. *Muscles Alive.* Baltimore: Williams and Wilkins, 1967.
2. Crouch, James E. *Functional Human Anatomy.* Philadelphia: Lea and Febiger, 1965.
3. deVries, Herbert A. *Physiology of Exercise for Physical Education and Athletics.* Dubuque, Iowa: Wm. C. Brown, 1966.
4. Edwards, Linder F. *Concise Anatomy.* New York: McGraw-Hill, 1956.
5. Falls, Harold B. (ed.). *Exercise Physiology.* New York: Academic Press, 1968.
6. Garden, John W., I. Wilson Dodd, and P. J. Rasch. "Acclimatization of Healthy Young Adult Males to a Hot-Wet Environment," *Journal of Applied Physiology,* 21 (March 1966), pp. 665-669.
7. Gaslen, R. V., B. Balke, F. J. Nagle, and E. E. Phillips. "Effects of Some Tranquilizing Analeptic and Vasodilating Drugs on Physical Work Capacity and Orthostatic Tolerance," *Aerospace Medicine,* 35 (July 19, 1964), pp. 630-633.

8. Golding, L. A., and R. J. Barnard. "The Effects of d-Amphetamine Sulfate on Physical Performance," *Journal of Sports Medicine and Physical Fitness,* 3 (December 1963), pp. 221-224.

9. Karpovich, Peter V. *Physiology of Muscular Activity.* Philadelphia: W. B. Saunders, 1965.

10. Lapp, Milton C., and Gink Gee. "Human Acclimatization to Cold Water Immersion—Effects on Physiological Activities," *Archives of Environmental Health,* 15 (November 1967), pp. 568-579.

11. Leary, W. P., and C. H. Wyndham. "Possible Effect on Athletic Performance of Mexico City's Altitude," *South African Medical Journal,* 40 (November 1966), pp. 984-985.

12. Matthews, Donald K., and Edward L. Fox. *The Physiological Basis of Physical Education and Athletics.* Philadelphia: W. B. Saunders, 1971.

13. Reeves, John T., Peter Jokl, and Jerome Coln. "Performance of Olympic Runners at Altitudes of 7,350 and 5,350 Feet," *The American Review of Respiratory Diseases,* 92 (November 1965), pp. 813-816.

14. Stern, M. H., and K. I. Melville. "A Comparative Evaluation of the Action of Depressant and Stimulant Drugs on Human Performance," *Psychopharmacologia,* 6 (1964), pp. 173-177.

15. Veghte, G. H., and Paul Webb. "Body Cooling and Response to Heat," *Journal of Applied Physiology,* 16 (March 1969), pp. 235-238.

foundations in the behavioral sciences

chapter 9

*The behavioral sciences are one of the major
intellectual and cultural inventions
of the twentieth century.*

BERNARD BERELSON

Just as it is necessary for the prospective physical educator to familiarize himself with the various biochemical, anatomical, and physiological principles so important to the discipline encompassing human movement, so is it necessary for him to become aware of the sociological and psychological principles which together constitute a part of the behavioral sciences.

The fields collectively embraced in what are termed the *behavioral sciences* represent a relatively new area of specialization, aimed primarily at under-standing human behavior. Each individual behaves as an individual; nevertheless, given certain sets of circumstances, the behavioral scientists can predict behavior patterns. Further, theories have been developed which explain certain human behavioral patterns with great accuracy. Regardless of the complexities surrounding it, human behavior can be researched scientifically.

The implications of the behavioral sciences for physical education are many and quite obvious. Sports situations often foster distinctive types of social behavior, and research that is being conducted increasingly in sports psychology and sports sociology helps to provide insight into such behavior. Why does a varsity team with all the physical requirements and skill to play well and win suffer through a disastrous season? Conversely, why does a participant who lacks what seem to be necessary physical attributes achieve success in a competitive situation in which he has no apparent chance? Why is the teacher confronted with different degrees of success in two different but supposedly homogeneous groups when he uses the same methodology with both? The answers to these questions fall within the purview of the behavioral sciences.

Since the behavioral sciences are of relatively recent origin, it is well to describe briefly their formulation and present status as well as to note their potential to physical education as a field of specialization. The broad term *social sciences* comprises three of the branches of learning which together make up the behavioral sciences: psychology, sociology, and anthropology. Berelson contends that any precise delineation of what constitutes the behavioral sciences is impossible. However, he states that two basic criteria must be met if a field is to be considered a part of the behavioral sciences: it must deal with human behavior, and it must conduct its study in a scientific manner to produce empirical, verifiable evidence.[1]

Examples of research in psychology which satisfy the above criteria include formulation of learning theory, exploration of personality, and experiments in communication. In sociology, the subject matter studied has included race relations and differing value orientations within a community. Analyses of cultural influences within and among ethnic groups are typical problems

---

1. Bernard Berelson (ed.), *The Behavioral Sciences Today* (New York: Harper and Row, 1964), p. 2.

researched in anthropology. There are obvious overlaps among the three areas, but they are probably desirable rather than otherwise, since they indicate common concern about mutual problems, not mere proliferation.

Examples of research problems in physical education by specialists in the three social sciences are the relationships between social class and activity preference, the effect of audience on individual performance, and the function of sports in various primitive and modern societies.

Although the *discipline* of behavioral science is structurally very young, the vast number of topics germane to it and the resulting expansion of knowledge have given rise to another area of specialized study—social psychology—which is of great interest to physical education and from which we can broaden our discipline's horizons. *Social psychology* is the experimental study of individuals and their behavioral dependence and interdependence in social and cultural settings. As the name implies, the specialist in this area delimits his concerns neither psychologically nor sociologically; instead he recognizes that human personality and behavior are results of both psychological processes and social influences. Social psychologists do not universally agree on a methodology for studying man's social nature, but they are unanimous in their conviction that they can, through careful study, reveal man's social nature and that such revelation will aid in understanding man in relation to the complex social forces acting upon him.[2]

How does the discipline of physical education relate to the discipline of social psychology? It is indeed interesting to note that the first experimental observation in social psychology, made in 1898 by Triplett, not only dealt with the effects of competition on human performance, but also involved recreational skills, namely, riding bicycles and winding fishing reels. Triplett's general finding was that competition facilitated performance, that individuals performed better in competition than alone. However, what he then called "competition" is today known as "social facilitation."[3] Three concerns that are important to the social psychologist are also very important to the physical educator: competition, cooperation, and conflict. Surely an insight into the characteristics of one or all of these behavior traits would be beneficial to specialists in both areas. The physical educator who is most concerned with human behavior in a sociocultural context may well pursue a specialization in social psychology in his graduate work.

Knowledge today is so complex and so intricate that no "strict disciplinar-

---

2. William W. Lambert and Wallace E. Lambert, *Social Psychology* (Englewood Cliffs, N.J.: Prentice-Hall, 1964), pp. 4-6.

3. Norman Triplett, "The Dynamogenic Factors of Pacemaking and Competition," *American Journal of Psychology*, 9 (1898), pp. 507-533.

ian" could ever research the innumerable ramifications of his discipline within narrow confines; nor would he wish to even if he could. The time is past when thoughtful academicians jealously guarded their discipline against what they considered encroachment by less well-prepared "outsiders." Reasonable men today realize that it is educationally desirable for different but related disciplines to conduct interdisciplinary investigations. Therefore, we find specialists within the discipline of physical education who, though primarily interested in physical education, have secondary interests that lie naturally within another and sometimes entirely different discipline. As an example, perhaps the relationship between the behavioral sciences and physical education is not so readily apparent as the relationship between medicine and physical education.

It is impossible in a book of this nature to explore fully the relationship between the behavioral sciences and physical education, but it is not impossible to help the beginning professional student in physical education become familiar with some of the more obvious connections between the two disciplines. Consequently, the remainder of this chapter will be devoted to a discussion of the history and current status of sports psychology and sports sociology and of selected principles from psychology and sociology, together with their application to physical education. No principles will be listed as social-psychological since such a category would cut across both fields, and the precise delineation they would require is beyond the scope of this book.

PSYCHOLOGY, SPORT PSYCHOLOGY, AND PSYCHOLOGICAL PRINCIPLES

Although the beginnings of psychology can perhaps be traced back to Plato and Aristotle and their discussions of mind-body relationships, experimental psychology as such is less than a century old. Many of the first problems scientifically researched revolved around theories of learning, motor learning, psychological conditioning, motivation, motor responses, and perception, all of which are also significant in physical education.

Sport psychology per se can also be traced back to the genesis of psychology as a discipline. However, much of the impetus in this area, particularly in the United States, has come about since World War II.[4] Sport psychologists today research such things as motivation, including the phenomenon of "psyching up" athletes (team arousal), and the role of personality in sports. Motivation to achieve success, for example, is not always predicated on a

---

4. Miroslav Vanek and Bryant J. Cratty, *Psychology and the Superior Athlete* (New York: Macmillan, 1970), pp. 3-32.

desire for the rewards which accrue to the winner; the motivation to avoid failure and its consequent unpleasantness is just as strong in some persons.[5]

As for the subject of arousing the emotions of a team, some sport psychologists today state that the relationship between arousal and performance is so complex that the coach is best advised not to experiment with techniques that may prove, if not actually harmful, at least not beneficial. Griffith, the "father of sport psychology," believed that emotional arousal did not affect performance positively, and he recorded that Knute Rockne, the fabled Notre Dame coach, agreed with this theory.[6] Ostensibly, however, this view is not shared by many of the foreign coaches and psychologists. Vanek and Cratty believe that "future records will be broken primarily because of increased attention to the psychological parameters of human personality."[7] It seems nonetheless apparent not only that different tasks demand different levels of arousal for the best performance, but that different personalities respond differently (sometimes adversely) to arousal. Since it is difficult to determine accurately the arousal level of an individual or a team at any given time, the need for research in these areas seems acute.[8] Future sport psychologists, take note! The potential contribution of such research to sports and organized athletics is monumental.[9]

Personality and its relationship to ability in sports is another area in which a high degree of research sophistication is needed. Physical educators and coaches, who have long expounded on the desirable personality traits exhibited by athletes, tend to imply that such traits are a result of participation in sports. Perhaps, however, these remarkable personality traits were present *before* participation. Again, future sport psychologists, take note!

It is probably correct to say that initial consideration of psychological theory by physical educators was along the lines of learning theories, principles, and "laws," as advocated by educational psychologists. This application was only natural in that the long-term concern of physical education was to prove that the two words which entitle our discipline are neither mutually exclusive nor contradictory.

---

5. Joe D. Willis and Don R. Bethe, "Achievement Motivation: Implications for Physical Activity," *Quest,* 13 (January 1970), pp. 18-22.

6. Walter Kroll and Guy Lewis, "America's First Sport Psychologist," *Quest,* 13 (January 1970), p. 2.

7. Vanek and Cratty, *op. cit.,* p. 4.

8. Joseph B. Oxendine, "Emotional Arousal and Motor Performance," *Quest,* 13 (January 1970), pp. 23-32.

9. Bryant J. Cratty, "Coaching Decisions and Research in Sport Psychology," *Quest,* 13 (January 1970), pp. 46-53.

Psychological Principles

A selected few of the psychological principles related to learning are described below, and an attempt is made to relate the application of each principle to physical education.

Individuals do not all learn at the same rate or in the same manner.

If this principle were not true, the teaching of any subject would be remarkably simple. Any brilliant educational psychologist could develop a teaching model with clearly defined directions, which any reasonably intelligent *technician* could follow with guaranteed results. However, the principle is true, and we therefore need to explore its many ramifications.

The key word is "individuals." Since every learner is an individual, he is cast from a unique mold. His personality, his environment, his innate intellectual as well as motor capacity—these are but examples of what makes him different from all others. Knowing that every person is unique but also that every learner experiences "plateaus" (leveling off in the learning curve where no further learning occurs) and "dips" (regressions) in learning, the wise teacher realizes the need for motivating the student so that the dips in the learning rate can be avoided and the length of the plateaus decreased. In physical education, the teacher may try rivalry as a motivating device, although he should be cognizant of the fact that the effectiveness of this technique decreases with the age of the learner. With a group of high school age, the teacher may try praise as a positive reinforcement to learning. For certain motor tasks, however, reproof has been demonstrated to facilitate learning more than praise. Unfortunately, not even the psychologist can predict which forms of motivation will work when and under what set of circumstances. Teaching, therefore, is not "remarkably simple"!

The learner repeats reactions which are satisfying and avoids those which are not.

This is the old "law of effect," which today might be more appropriately discussed under a "reinforcement" theory. Indeed, the statement is so true that it hardly requires explanation, but as oftens happens, it may be overlooked simply because it is obvious.

For example, some football coaches, usually neophytes in the coaching ranks, are so imbued with a "let's-separate-the-men-from-the-boys" attitude that they conduct vigorous physical scrimmages almost from the beginning of the football season. The coach who does so fails to realize that there are undoubtedly some boys, at least among his beginners, who are not yet certain whether they like physical contact. To expose them to such contact too soon may make some of them decide not to continue in football. A more reasonable coach brings his boys along slowly and tries to make each practice session satisfying. Thereby he more nearly ensures that potentially good players will remain with football long enough to achieve their potential. A more dramatic example of the working of this principle is the beginning swimmer who "almost drowns." Once such an unpleasant experience has occurred, it is difficult for the learner to reenter the water and enjoy learning to swim.

A reaction will not transfer to all situations.

Again, if this statement were not true, teaching would be considerably easier. An insightful learner *may* see the relationship between skill in different activities, and insight is positively correlated with intelligence. Regardless of the intelligence level of the individual, however, he can profit from teacher guidance in the matter of transfer.

In physical education there seems to be a direct relationship between skill components of, say, an overhand softball throw and a tennis serve. Why, then, should not the teacher cite this relationship to the individual having difficulty with the tennis serve? There is a strong chance that this same learner has long since learned the overhand throw. The application of this principle seems to be that if the teacher wants transfer to occur, he should teach for it. Such teaching can take two forms. In the first and most desirable form, an individual can be taught in such a way that cognitive outcomes are ensured from the beginning of his organized physical education instruction. Thus he *understands* the mechanical principles underlying efficient movement, and he is able to apply them to any new situation. However, even if an individual has been taught this way, he sometimes has trouble with a new skill for any one of a number of reasons. Therefore, the teacher may on occasion have to resort to the second form of teaching and point out the similarities in the two skills. Direct teaching, or what Mosston refers to as "command" teaching, cannot always be avoided.[10]

Habit represents an important factor in learning.

All learning theories deal in one way or another with habit, whether they are behavioristic-connectionist theories, with their emphasis on conditioning, or cognitive-field theories, with their emphasis on conceptual processes. One can assume that the various behavioristic theories place greater stress on habit formation, but in any case, repetition of a motor task is essential if performance of the task is to become automatic.

Insofar as physical education is concerned, automatic or habitual motor responses at the lower level of skill development are no doubt desirable. This circumstance explains the emphasis on drill that characterizes much of the

10. Muska Mosston, *Teaching Physical Education: From Command to Discovery* (Columbus, Ohio: Charles E. Merrill, 1966).

teaching seen in the gymnasium or on the playing fields. However, for more complex motor tasks, dependence on habitual response alone is sheer folly. If automatic performance of a complex task depends on the existence of a certain combination of external conditions, the wise teacher recognizes the necessity for stressing cognitive concepts and alternative responses, because that particular combination of conditions of the external environment may very seldom occur.

In basketball, for example, we often find players who have not only favorite shots but favorite spots on the floor from which to shoot. The intelligent coach, whether or not he is working with a patterned offense, not only teaches his squad variations of "plays" but even goes so far as to have his guards double-team the player who always wants to get to that favorite spot before shooting. Since the coach recognizes that the opposing coach may be teaching exactly the same strategy, he tries to prepare his player for the fact that his pet shot from a pet spot will not always work. In other words, the coach tries to get his players to understand and conceptualize the different situations as they occur on the floor and to adjust to them accordingly.

Psychological tensions are produced by certain situations.

There is some degree of tension in any learning situation. However, some individuals reach much more quickly than others the level of tension that minimizes learning or even precludes it. Such factors as noise, physical condition, temperature of the room, emotional status, personality, and presence of others contribute to tension in varying degrees.

The wise teacher should be aware of rising tension, whether in one individual, a few, or the entire class. He also needs to know what to do about it, but unfortunately, there is no universal solution. From experience the teacher learns to know each individual better, and thus he becomes more able to cope with the situation. For example, he may talk to an individual away from the group, completely change the learning activity, or strive to adjust physical factors to improve the environment.

Learning is a process of experiencing and reacting to a variety of situations.

This principle is of great importance in all cognitive-field theories of learning, but it is valid in the behavioristic theories as well. No learning situation can be so isolated that other situations do not enter the total picture. Even those theoreticians who believe in the part method of teaching skill admit that the learning of isolated component parts does not always produce an effective performance in the whole (game) situation. It therefore seems wise for the physical educator to teach in gamelike situations.

"Gamelike" does not mean throwing the ball out and just letting the learners play, however. It implies a concerted effort on the part of the teacher to help the learner conceptualize the relationship between the "parts" and the "whole." It further means that, on occasion, practice of a skill is conducted under conditions that duplicate as closely as possible the actual game situation. For example, to keep practicing the bully in field hockey with only the two center forwards involved is rather futile when, in a game situation, the "bullyer" is immediately confronted by several other girls.

The psychological principles presented here are only a few of the many principles that are germane to the work of the teacher-coach. As the student of physical education delves more deeply into his professional studies, he should gain greater knowledge of psychology and thus greater insight into the psychological principles which undergird teaching. As Scott[11] so well states, the physical educator is a "practical psychologist," who contributes to the following psychological outcomes as well as to skill acquisition: changed attitudes, improved social efficiency, improved mental health, improved sensory perception and responses, and improved ability to relax.

SOCIOLOGY, SPORT SOCIOLOGY, AND SOCIOLOGICAL PRINCIPLES

A recent and significant book edited by Loy and Kenyon[12] constitutes the first attempt to bring together in English a representative sampling of the wide variety of studies relating to both sociology and physical education that are being conducted throughout the world. Much of the background in the present section comes from the diversified articles contained in that volume. Anyone interested in more complete information about the sociology of sports will find that book a valuable source.

Sociology can be defined as the "scientific study of society, its structure, functions, and processes."[13] It can be divided into three broad fields: study of groups, analysis of institutions, and study of general social structure. Although the "discipline" was founded in the nineteenth century, those features which make sociology truly a discipline—rigorous scientific methodology, behavioral orientation, conceptual consciousness—are to a great extent the product of the past fifty years.[14]

Currently sociologists are very active in researching various problems that

---

11. M. Gladys Scott, "The Contributions of Physical Activity to Psychological Development," in H. S. Slusher and A. S. Lockhart (eds.), *Anthology of Contemporary Readings* (Dubuque, Iowa: W. C. Brown, 1970), p. 130.

12. John W. Loy, Jr., and Gerald S. Kenyon (eds.), *Sport, Culture, and Society* (New York: Macmillan, 1969).

13. Harry S. Alpert, "Sociology: Its Present Interests," in B. Berelson (ed.), *The Behavioral Sciences Today* (New York: Harper and Row, 1964), p. 53.

14. *Ibid.*, p. 52.

come under the general classification of group study, such as types of social groups, patterns of relationships between and among groups, bases on which groups are formulated, and attitudes within groups. Sociological research in the field of institutional analysis has fostered the formulation of ideas concerning, for example, the persistence of such basic institutions as the family, the interdependence of institutions as seen from the fact that change in one presages changes in others, and the tendency of groups to perpetuate themselves. Social structure in general can best be understood by a careful appraisal of the social classes within the overall structure. Along these lines, sociologists have been researching such factors as expected behavior characteristics within classes, stresses that arise between classes, and mobility between and within classes.[15]

One can easily see how the concerns above are related to a study of sports, play, and games, and thus one can readily understand that a subdiscipline known as sport sociology soon established itself in the academic community.

Some of the early leaders in the field of physical education in the United States mentioned in Chapter 1, such as Hetherington and Williams, asserted social objectives for physical education as early as the turn of this century. However, there were few early attempts by social scientists to study sports, which make up one of our most common yet least understood social institutions. Most of the scientific study in this area has been conducted within the past 20 to 25 years. The efforts have not been confined to the United States; in fact, serious study of play, sports, and games in foreign countries preceded similar activity here.

Sociological literature pertaining to sports is not confined to sociologists or physical educators. Indeed, a recent article by Bill Russell, the basketball great, has sociological, psychological, and philosophical overtones.[16] And of course, journalistic literature abounds in discussions of the relationships of sports to society.

In 1959 the International Council of Sport and Physical Education was formed, and in 1964 that UNESCO-sponsored body appointed a Committee on Sport Sociology. The committee comprises both physical educators and sociologists, and the programs its members support have exhibited a diversified international flavor and continue to do so. The committee has sponsored international seminars, and it coordinates international research on the subject as well as publishes *The International Review of Sport Sociology*.

The number of persons in the United States who might properly be called sport sociologists is small; however, there is encouraging evidence that interest in

---

15. *Ibid.*, pp. 54-57.
16. William F. Russell, "Success is a Journey," *Sports Illustrated*, **32**:23 (June 8, 1970), pp. 80-88, 93.

this subdiscipline is growing in the fact that the number of institutions of higher learning that offer specialized study in the area, both at the master's and the doctoral level, is increasing. That the field of sociology per se is accepting the sport sociologist as a well-prepared disciplinarian is in turn demonstrated by the fact that there is also an increase in the number of courses cross-listed in departments of physical education and sociology that are being taught by physical educators.

Of the almost limitless possibilities for research in the area, just a few are cited below.

1. The role of sports and games in influencing value systems and the converse. For example, has the "All-American" hero type vanished with the emergence of the professional athlete who sees his role strictly in business terms?

2. Influences of sports on family life. Many people believe that the family that prays together stays together. Many physical educators would like to believe as well that the family that *plays* together stays together. Is this true?

3. Social phenomena surrounding sports events. How do social phenomena differ with different events? For example, contrast a boxing match with, say, a "tailgate" picnic prior to an Ivy League football game.

4. The role of politics and government in athletic endeavors. Should governments subsidize Olympic competitors? Should the International Olympic Committee ban any nation from competing because of its internal political structure?

5. The role of sports in developing countries. Why does the Peace Corps recruit so heavily among physical educators and athletes?

6. Crowd behavior. Why is an unruly mob "tolerated" after a big football victory, when the same mob actions in different situations would earn for the participating college-age youths the label of "radicals"?

7. Values in sports that serve as instruments for the social good. Has the rise of organized sports in the United States lessened intolerance and discrimination?

Sociological Principles

As before when dealing with the psychological aspects of the behavioral sciences spectrum, we now offer a selected few sociological principles together with their application to physical education. Though limited, the list is fairly representative.

The social situation influences the learning process.

The child in a learning situation is confronted by many social factors, some of them contradictory. In the matter of value orientation alone, for example, an educator or family member who espouses the value of honesty may on occasion be observed in dishonest behavior. What is the child to conclude in regard to his own actions?

The physical educator must not only teach those social values deemed desirable in our culture but practice them under all circumstances.

Peer-group attitudes are important behavior-forming influences.

That this statement is more true at certain maturation stages than at others is uncontestable. Peer-group influence is usually at its height at the junior high school level, when the importance to each individual of being accepted by his peers tends to be so great that he will conform to expected behavior patterns, even if he questions them, in order to maintain status in the group. This phenomenon explains such diverse things as fads in clothing and hair styles or the conforming to certain moral standards, even though they are contrary to deep-seated religious convictions.

The role the leader of the peer group plays can be crucial. If he has values that society defines as desirable, no problem exists. If he has values that point in the opposite direction, however, it is the duty of the physical educator to try to change the leader's value system, thereby influencing the entire group. For example, a leader who feels that a certain activity is too "square" can influence his group to resist it. Unfortunately, many athletic coaches today are faced with the job of "selling" interscholastic participation.

Each person should have an opportunity for self-realization within bounds that society deems desirable.

Self-realization has always been an objective in American education—an objective that often receives only lip service. Today, with the behavioral sciences stressing the importance of self-realization, many people believe that society is going overboard in not only allowing but encouraging everyone "to do his own thing." Experience in similar circumstances suggests that vacillating from one end of the conformity-permissiveness continuum to the other is unproductive. Such a procedure, in fact, often leads not only to a more perplexed and perhaps less stable individual but also to a society seemingly without direction.

The implication for the physical educator, then, is clear although his task is nonetheless difficult. He must provide the individual with an opportunity for genuine self-realization. Perhaps he can best do this by offering a wide variety of activities in his program so that each individual can find at least one in which he can excel. Lessening the stress on the authoritarian teaching which has characterized our field should also prove beneficial in the implementation of self-realization.

Education should stress the concept of sharing.

The United States is a nation of contrasts, not the least of which is great wealth and abject poverty. If American society values the concept of sharing, education must do more than merely provide lip service about it. The various fields in education must provide opportunities for sharing and must stress the value cognitively so that the transfer of sharing from one situation to another is enhanced.

Physical education, with its long stressed concept of teamwork, is a particularly good field in which to meet this objective. However, if sharing is to become truly a behavorial outcome and not merely a paper objective, physical educators need to point out how teamwork can logically transfer to other life situations, in spite of the fact that transfer is usually situation-specific. There are many instances in sports in which victory depends on subordinating oneself for the good of the group—sacrificing in baseball, passing off to a teammate in basketball, setting up for a spike in volleyball. In these instances, race, color, creed, and economic status, to cite just a few factors, are immaterial. Why shouldn't they be immaterial in life?

Education should help each individual adjust successfully to changing social conditions.

Perhaps the need for such help has never been more obvious than in today's society. Not only is there a "generation gap," but there seems also to be sincere confusion about standards and values among school-age individuals in an existentially oriented environment. Education must rise to the challenge and become an effective tool for ameliorating seeming conflicts.

If physical education is to fit into this changed social order, the curriculum must escape the traditional, repetitive, practical approach and develop an orientation toward more diversified exploration of human movement. Perhaps the current emphasis on movement education and problem-solving methodology are steps in this direction. Along with a change in the program of activities must come a change in the philosophy regarding the learner's role in the educative process. Youth needs to be taught how to cope intelligently with differing viewpoints, differing abilities, differing life styles. What better place to do this than the laboratory-activity sessions that characterize much of the learning process in physical education, where there is truly an intermingling of many and diverse personalities and viewpoints? In contrast to the too typical classroom situation where social problems are merely verbalized, the physical education laboratory affords an opportunity to put theory into practice.

The principles we have cited here, though few in number, are representative of those sociological precepts which the physical educator should use to guide his actions when dealing with possible social learning. These selected principles should assume additional importance as the prospective teacher's exposure to the study of sociology becomes broader and more diversified.

SUMMARY

Physical educators have long advocated that desirable social and psychological traits are natural outcomes from work in the discipline. Although such claims seem to have merit, research into cause and effect relationships is greatly needed to establish the validity of assumptions about the behavioral consequences of participation in physical education and sports.

Research into the psychology of physical education and sports is needed to provide insight into such diverse psychological manisfestations as motivation; emotional arousal and its effects on performance; self-actualization and all its contiguous aspects, such as ego fulfillment, self-perception, etc.; the role of play in mental health; theories of play; the attraction of spectator sports; cooperation versus competition; eu-stress versus dys-stress;[17] and personality.

Personality factors have interested physical educators for many years and continue to be the subject of psychological research in physical education. However, such research in the past has left much to be desired in terms of rigorous scientific methodology, and therefore the conclusions have been, at best, generalized and superficial.[18] There is hope that this situation is changing, because physical educators with specialized training in psychology are beginning to realize that there is a vast, untapped well of insight into the complexities of personality and physical activity waiting to be revealed by sophisticated research. Many universities today are offering courses in motor learning and the psychology of sports. Furthermore, the founding in 1965 of the North American Society of Psychology in Sport and Physical Activity, which sponsors national and international congresses of sports psychology,[19] is an indication that this speciality within the discipline of physical education has established itself.

Snyder,[20] a sociologist engaged in research on aspects of the sociology of sports, states that the dimensions of social interaction in the socialization process must be analyzed in order to understand whether the influence of

17. Dorothy V. Harris, "On the Brink of Catastrophe," *Quest,* 13 (January 1970), pp. 33-40.

18. Pearl Berlin, "Prolegomena to the Study of Personality by Physical Educators," *Quest,* 13 (January 1970), pp. 54-63.

19. Vanek and Cratty, *op. cit.,* pp. 23-24.

20. Eldon E. Snyder, "Aspects of Socialization in Sports and Physical Education," *Quest,* 14 (June 1970), pp. 1-7.

participation in physical education and sports activities can be diffused beyond a specific situation. The following dimensions in the specific situational context are among the most important, according to Snyder.

1. The participants' degree of involvement in the activity. There is usually greater involvement in a varsity sport than in a physical education class. The coach and captain of a particular varsity team also tend to be more deeply involved than substitute players are.

2. Voluntary or involuntary selection of and participation in an activity. Participation in varsity sports is usually voluntary, whereas participation in the physical education program is required. One would expect the voluntary activity to foster greater involvement and thus a more diffused socialization.

3. Instrumental or socialization relationships. This dimension relates to the quality of the relationship between participants and socializing agents. Instrumental relationships can be thought of as largely utilitarian with no intervening variables. In contrast, socialization relationships foster genuine interplay among participants and are thus personally satisfying ends in themselves. Socialization relationships are difficult, if not impossible, to encourage in a traditionally taught class in physical education. The teacher who is concerned with developing this type of relationship needs to be cognizant of the shortcomings of the "traditional" method of teaching.

4. The power and prestige of the teacher or coach. It seems obvious that the higher the esteem in which the teacher is held, the greater his influence will be. Power is akin to esteem or prestige, and generally speaking, the person who is held in high esteem also exerts great control over the participants.

5. Social and personal characteristics of the participants. Such traits as physical talent, mental ability, and self-perception are important in the diffusion of behavioral outcomes; nevertheless, such variables as social class and ethnic affiliations[21] must not be overlooked.

Snyder concludes by asserting that physical educators must understand the socialization process that occurs in physical education and that attention to this consideration must receive high priority within the discipline.

Just as psychology and sociology of physical education and sports have emerged as recognized subdisciplines of their parent disciplines, so social psychology as an interdisciplinary field has become of extreme importance in the body of knowledge germane to the discipline of physical education.

---

21. John C. Pooley, "Ethnic Soccer Clubs in Milwaukee: A Study in Assimilation," research paper read at the AAHPER annual convention, Boston, April 11, 1969.

Martens[22] contends that social psychology is primarily concerned with the process of social influence and that as an area of study it is distinct from either psychology or sociology in that it is primarily interested in understanding the social-influence processes underlying the *individual* as a participant in social relationships.

In conclusion, the social sciences which together constitute the behavioral sciences abound in research possibilities in physical education and sports. However, only when physical educators use the particular research designs and techniques rigorously and well will we be able to do more than conjecture about the interrelationships among those disciplines interested in man and his activity.

---

22. Rainer Martens, "A Social Psychology of Physical Activity," *Quest,* **14** (June 1970), pp. 8-17.

STUDENT PROJECTS

1. Interview various coaches at both the high school and college level to determine whether they believe in "psyching up" their teams. If they do, what methods do they use? If they do not believe in it, why not?

2. Repeat the above with several varsity players.

3. Report on at least one *research* study on the general topic of personality of the athlete.

4. What sports in the United States seem to have ethnic connotations? Why?

5. Select some good bowlers and some nonbowlers from the class. Have both groups bowl one line without an audience and record their scores. Repeat with the entire class as an audience. Observe the results and try to explain them.

6. Divide the class into two groups. Have the members of the first group throw bean bags ten feet over their shoulders into a waste basket. Record the number of successes in a ten-second time span. Immediately repeat the test twice. Now have the second group perform the same test, but give them a five-minute break between test trials. Observe the results and try to explain them.

GLOSSARY OF TERMS

Behavioral sciences Those fields which attempt to understand human behavior: psychology, sociology, and anthropology.

Social psychology The study of the influences that produce regularities and diversities in human social behavior.

Sport psychology The study of the influences that produce regularities and diversities of human behavior in physical activity and sports settings.

Sport sociology The study of sports as a social and cultural phenomenon.

Competition A striving by two or more individuals or teams for one goal. As one individual or team moves toward that goal, the possibility that the others will reach it decreases.

Contest A striving by two or more units (individuals or teams) for superiority under well-defined rules and mutual agreement.

Team arousal An attempt to motivate a team to perform well, often called "psyching up."

SELECTED REFERENCES

1. Alpert, Harry S. "Sociology: Its Present Interests," in B. Berelson (ed.), *The Behavioral Sciences Today*. New York: Harper and Row, 1964.

2. Berelson, Bernard (ed.). *The Behavioral Sciences Today*. New York: Harper and Row, 1964.

3. Berlin, Pearl. "Prolegomena to the Study of Personality by Physical Educators," *Quest*, **13** (January 1970).

4. Bethe, Don R., and Joe D. Willis. "Achievement Motivation: Implications for Physical Activity," *Quest*, **13** (January 1970).

5. Bookwalter, Karl W., and Harold J. VanderZwaag. *Foundations and Principles of Physical Education*. Philadelphia: W. B. Saunders, 1969.

6. Committee of Sport Sociology of the International Council of Sport and Physical Education (ed.), *International Review of Sport Sociology*, Vols. 1, 2, 3. Warsaw: Polish Scientific, 1966, 1967, 1968.

7. Cratty, Bryant J. "Coaching Decisions and Research in Sport Psychology," *Quest*, **13** (January 1970), pp. 46-53.

8. Frost, Reuben B. *Psychological Concepts Applied to Physical Education and Coaching*. Reading, Mass.: Addison-Wesley, 1971.

9. Harris, Dorothy V. "On the Brink of Catastrophe," *Quest*, **13** (January 1970).

10. Husman, Burris F. "Sport in Personality Dynamics," *Proceedings*, National College Association of Physical Education for Men (1969), pp. 56-70.

11. Jokl, Ernst, and E. Simon (eds.). *International Research in Sport and Physical Education*. Springfield, Ill.: Charles C. Thomas, 1964.

12. Kroll, Walter, and Guy M. Lewis. "America's First Sport Psychologist," *Quest*, **13** (January 1970).

13. Lambert, William W., and Wallace E. Lambert. *Social Psychology*. Englewood Cliffs, N.J.: Prentice-Hall, 1964.

14. Loy, John W., Jr., and Gerald S. Kenyon (eds.). *Sport, Culture and Society*. New York: Macmillan, 1969.

15. McIntosh, Peter C. *Sport in Society*. London: C. A. Watts, 1963.

16. Maheu, Rene. "Sport and Culture," *Journal of Health, Physical Education and Recreation*, **34** (October 1963), pp. 30-32.

17. Martens, Rainer. "A Social Psychology of Physical Activity," *Quest*, **14** (June 1970).

18. Morgan, William P. (ed.). *Contemporary Readings in Sport Psychology*. Springfield, Ill.: Charles C. Thomas, 1970.

19. Mosston, Muska. *Teaching Physical Education: From Command to Discovery*. Columbus, Ohio: Charles E. Merrill, 1966.

20. Nixon, John E., and Ann E. Jewett. *An Introduction to Physical Education.* Philadelphia: W. B. Saunders, 1969.

21. Oxendine, Joseph B. "Emotional Arousal and Motor Performance," *Quest,* **13** (January 1970).

22. Resick, Matthew C., Beverly L. Seidel, and James Mason. *Modern Administrative Practices in Physical Education and Athletics.* Reading, Mass.: Addison-Wesley, 1970.

23. Russell, William F. "Success is a Journey," *Sports Illustrated,* **32** (June 8, 1970).

24. Sage, George H. *Introduction to Motor Behavior.* Reading, Mass.: Addison-Wesley, 1971.

25. Scott, M. Gladys. "The Contributions of Physical Activity to Psychological Development," in H. S. Slusher and A. S. Lockhart (eds.), *Anthology of Contemporary Readings.* Dubuque, Iowa: W. C. Brown, 1970, pp. 129-144.

26. Slusher, Howard S., and Ailene S. Lockhart (eds.). *Anthology of Contemporary Readings.* Dubuque: W. C. Brown, 1970.

27. Snyder, Eldon E. "Aspects of Socialization in Sports and Physical Education," *Quest,* **14** (June 1970).

28. Triplett, Norman. "The Dynamogenic Factors of Pacemaking and Competition," *American Journal of Psychology,* **9** (1898), pp. 507-533.

29. Vanek, Miroslav, and Bryant J. Cratty. *Psychology and the Superior Athlete.* New York: Macmillan, 1970.

30. White, Cyril M. "Towards a Sociology of Physical Education and Sport, Some Theoretical Considerations," in H. S. Slusher and A. S. Lockhart (eds.), *Anthology of Contemporary Readings.* Dubuque, Iowa: W. C. Brown, 1970.

31. Zajonc, Robert B. *Social Psychology: An Experimental Approach.* Belmont, Calif.: Wadsworth, 1966.

athletics in school and society

chapter 10

Participation in sound athletic programs, we believe, contributes to health and happiness, physical skill and emotional maturity, social competence and moral values.

EDUCATIONAL POLICIES COMMISSION,
NATIONAL EDUCATION ASSOCIATION

The place of athletics in society, but more particularly in the schools, is an issue which has been debated for many years. Arguments from its proponents at one end of the value continuum espouse for athletics the same objectives as for all of education. Its detractors at the other end of the continuum insist that athletics is merely one aspect of show business and, as such, should be divorced from the American educational enterprise. No doubt each of these viewpoints has some merit. A program of athletics properly conducted has invaluable and almost limitless opportunities for meeting many of the objectives which education deems desirable. On the other hand, the same program improperly conducted can in no way be evaluated as educational, and therefore the "show business" connotation is probably appropriate. Why is there such a divergence of viewpoints about the school program of athletics? Perhaps the best way to answer this question is to trace briefly the development of organized athletics; to discuss the present school program, its values and its problems; and finally, to digest current trends and assess the future. Although the treatment is school-oriented, the role of athletics in society has an influence on the school program and vice versa.

HISTORY OF ORGANIZED ATHLETICS

The early settlers brought some sports and games with them to the New World, but there was very little in the way of organized athletics in the communities and none in the schools until after the first quarter of the nineteenth century.

There is less than complete agreement on the specific origins of many sports and games, but the following statements regarding three of America's better-known sports activities are generally accepted.

Baseball, America's so-called national game, evolved from cricket and rounders, and both Doubleday and Cartwright are given some credit for its invention or development. The first organized team was the Knickerbocker Baseball Club of New York, founded in 1845. The first college game was played between Amherst and Williams in 1859.

The present game of American football developed directly from soccer and indirectly from rugby. Although the National Collegiate Athletic Association (NCAA) celebrated the hundredth anniversary of football in 1969, in all probability, the 1869 game between Rutgers and Princeton was a soccer game.

The invention of basketball by Naismith in 1891 filled a need for a game that could be played indoors during the long winter months, when football, soccer, and baseball could not be played.

While these and other sports were developing, the European programs of physical education were being introduced into American schools. Sports activities were conducted in the schools by the citizens of the community and by unsupervised high school and university students. School played school, town played town,• and many a playing field at times took on the look of a battleground. Football evolved into an especially rough sport, and the games became so dangerous that they were abolished for years by the faculties of Harvard and Yale. This roughness had reached a climax by the year 1905, when President Theodore Roosevelt called a meeting of representatives from Yale, Princeton, and Harvard to discuss the future of the game. That action can be considered the first real attempt to control athletic programs.

Beginnings of athletic controls

In spite of the difficulties encountered, athletics developed rapidly and by 1879 had reached such proportions that there arose a need for some kind of control. A direct result was the formation of the National Association of Amateur Athletes of America, an organization which developed into the Amateur Athletic Union (AAU) in 1888.

In 1905 the Chancellor of New York University, Henry McCracken, called a meeting of the nation's colleges to decide the fate of college football. Twenty-eight colleges were represented, and the groundwork was laid for the formation of the present National Collegiate Athletic Association (NCAA), founded in 1910. The most important agreement reached was that the conduct of athletics was to be left to the discretion of duly authorized school authorities, but such aspects as recruiting, subsidization, schedules, and tournaments were to be controlled.

In order to effect such control, most schools formed athletic boards of control or athletic councils. This type of administrative arrangement still operates on many college campuses and in many secondary schools. In the years that followed the formation of the AAU and the NCAA, interest not only in participating in but also in watching sports was highly evident among students and citizens of the communities. The affluence that followed World War I increased this interest. A Carnegie Foundation report entitled *American College Athletics,* issued in 1929, disclosed a shocking turn toward professionalism in all aspects of college sports.[1] The disclosure of scandals in recruiting athletes and subsidizing them by means of scholarships threatened the very existence of athletics in the school program. Athletic conferences were forced into a policing action in order to survive. Shortly after this report was issued, however, the

---

1. Howard J. Savage, *American College Athletics,* Bulletin 23 (New York: Carnegie Foundation for the Advancement of Teaching, 1929).

United States suffered through the "Great Depression," and the drastic changes in the economy that followed served to remove the pressure of the critical issues facing competitive athletics. There have been minor athletic scandals since that period but perhaps nothing to match the disclosures in 1929.

NCAA-AAU conflicts

In recent years both the NCAA and the AAU have developed into powerful organizations for the control of amateur athletics. The NCAA was formed to promote college and university athletic programs, whereas the AAU deals with amateur athletic programs outside educational institutions. Under the circumstances, there seems to be little ground for dissent, but problems do arise in the selection of teams and coaches to take part in international competition, including the Olympics. The AAU has the official approval of the International Olympic Committee to select team members, team coaches, meet sites, and times. However, the training ground for many of the activities is the college and university athletic program. Furthermore, many of the athletes competing for team membership are attending colleges and universities on athletic grants-in-aid, and at times the NCAA and AAU codes are in conflict. Unfortunately, the student athlete suffers. The problems are not insurmountable, but they are significant enough to have fostered governmental intervention at the federal level. One must hope, for the good of organized sport, both at home and abroad, that reasonable men will come together and resolve their conflicts.

EDUCATIONAL VALUES
OF INTERSCHOOL ATHLETICS

The instructional program in physical education is an integral part of the curricular offerings of any school. And the field of physical education can point with pride to the fact that it was one of the first areas to extend its offerings into co-curricular activities, such as intramurals, extramurals, and varsity sports. All of these programs can lay claim to meeting particular and individualized needs of students.

The intramural program, largely sports-oriented, is conducted "within the walls" of a particular educational institution. Its participants are usually semiskilled individuals, interested in engaging to a greater extent in some of the activities learned in the physical education class. Hence intramurals are often referred to as the physical education laboratory.

Extramural participation extends beyond a specific school, but usually competition in this category is informally organized and conducted. An example of extramural competition is a sports day in which two or more schools compete

Gymnasts display the skill necessary for varsity competition. Photo courtesy of Kent State University Gymnastics Team.

against each other in one or more activities. The teams from the schools are not of varsity caliber, but they may be the intramural winners in a particular sport in their respective schools.

The varsity team is a highly select group, representing a superior skill level, which receives extra coaching for the purpose of engaging in an interschool program of competitive athletics. It is in varsity athletics that the exceptional student has the opportunity to develop his talent further and to measure himself against other similarly gifted individuals. The varsity athlete is somewhat like the student who develops his speaking ability and enters forensic contests, the student musician who is a member of the concert band, and the student thespian who stars in school dramatic productions.

Many values are possible outcomes of such programs, but none can be guaranteed, of course. If the leadership is sound and if the program is kept within a justifiable educational perspective, the following values—in addition to the obvious ones revolving around physical fitness and a healthy body skilled in movement—seem to be possible outcomes from participation in athletics.

1. Moral and social values. It is possible to learn fair play, courage, justice, democratic skills, etc., in an atmosphere where social class, religion, color, and creed pale into insignificance as *human* values shine brightly through. Competition, conflict, and cooperation are all inherent in our society. In a wisely conducted program of interschool athletics, competitive and cooperative behavior can be maximized while conflict is at the same time being minimized.

2. Intellectual values. The opportunities to think critically and constructively are unparalleled in competitive athletics, in which there is constant need to make decisions with physical, social, and moral ramifications.

3. Emotional values. In a society in which pressures and tensions are so great that emotional illness is a national problem, it is helpful to be able to learn to adjust to pressure in a game situation. In addition, self-perception of one's body image—in other words, feeling at home in one's own body—is necessary for psychological well-being.

4. Cultural values. Using the body as a means of creative self-expression is today recognized to be just as "cultural" as expressing oneself through such other media as art, music, and drama.

5. Vocational values. A program of interschool athletics can serve as a

Football combines individual effort with teamwork. Photo courtesy of Kent ▶
State University Athletic Department.

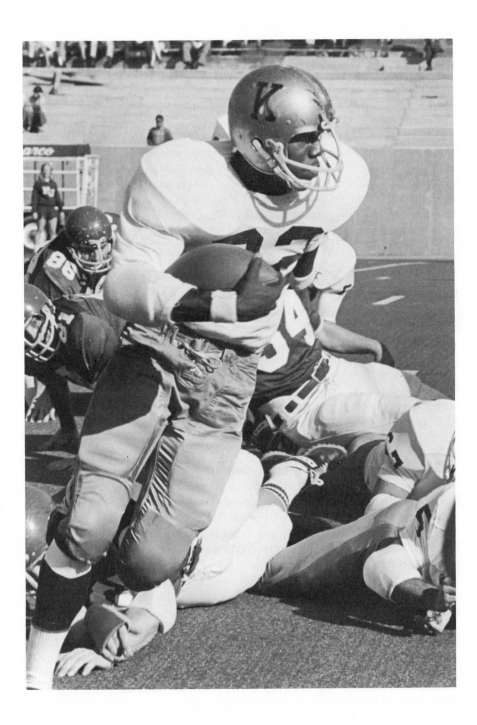

vocational laboratory for future physical educators, coaches, and professional athletes. In addition, many of the attributes learned in such a program are important to later success in other vocational pursuits.

Thus most, if not all, of the objectives inherent in education are obtainable in a well-rounded, diversified curricular and co-curricular program of physical education. However, the interschool program in competitive athletics, theoretically the culmination of a sound instructional program in physical education, seems often to have received undue emphasis—to such an extent that the entire program, including interschool competition, is in danger of collapse. No area of study deserves the title "educational" if it uses most of its resources, human and otherwise, to serve the talented minority. What, then, are some of the problem areas in interschool athletic programs, and what can be done to eliminate them?

THE PROBLEMS IN ATHLETICS

Because athletics are an integral part of the community and a rallying point for both school and community spirit, the values in athletics too often become distorted. The distortion may begin in the school with a coach who sometimes *uses* athletes as stepping stones to further his own coaching career. It is helped along by the school's administrative echelon, which makes one set of rules for athletes and another set for the remainder of the student body. The distortion is further nurtured by the community, which demands victory over the neighboring community—even to the point of insisting that a coach be fired if the wins do not greatly exceed the losses. And finally, the pressure comes from those parents who enjoy the vicarious thrill of athletic success by sharing the glory of victory with sons and daughters who are team members.

Another problem arises from the fact that the interschool athletic program, as an extra or co-curricular activity, must be largely if not entirely self-sustaining financially. Thus it is mandatory to have good gate receipts, and seemingly, this result can be accomplished only by fielding winning teams. In order to ensure that goal, action is taken which brings about many of the abuses of the program: lax eligibility standards, improper recruiting, illegal subsidizing, and other unethical coaching practices.

Yet another nagging question relative to keeping the program in an education perspective revolves around the age and grade level at which interschool sports should be initiated. Although selfish perpetuators of the feeder system would begin the process in kindergarten, there is no supportive evidence to indicate either that a need exists for interscholastic athletic programs

Basketball, a game for the well-coordinated and well-conditioned athlete. Photo ▶ courtesy of Kent State University Athletic Department.

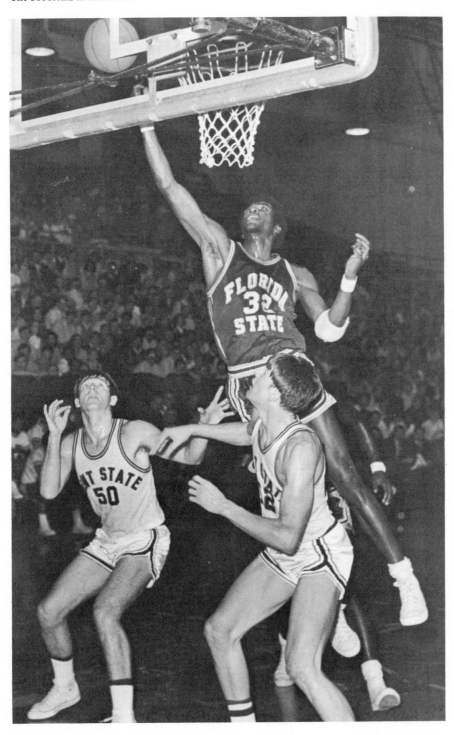

at the elementary school level or that such early participation produces superior athletes at a later date. Nevertheless, the argument that outside agencies sponsor it (for example, Little League baseball and Peewee football) seems sufficient to sway the administration in some school systems. Overlooked is the fact that such programs are adult-inspired, adult-motivated, and adult-controlled. Such programs do not permit children to enjoy the discovery and thrill of play in an unstructured atmosphere, and at the same time they severely limit participation. A strong intramural program permits the participation and development of all who wish to compete. In the long run, this practice is productive of a better interschool program.

The program of interscholastic athletics at the junior high school level is so entrenched that it is now almost unquestionably accepted in spite of research evidence which militates against *unrestricted* programs, especially in the contact sports. Much research is still needed concerning injuries to the bones during periods of growth and concerning the possibilities that interference with normal growth patterns can be traced to competitive athletics. Just as important is the unanswered question of the result of the emotional impact on young students due to tensions in competitive situations. Since it is unlikely that these programs will cease, it is mandatory that properly educated teacher-coaches be placed in positions of responsibility for their organization and administration.

Perhaps the biggest problem in interscholastic athletics at the senior high school level is that the program is so firmly entrenched in the minds and hearts of the citizens of the community that it is difficult for them to consider sports as education or as recreation. Instead they view the program as entertainment, and since they have such a vested interest in it and its participants, they tend to compare it to professional programs or at least to successful college programs. The National Federation of State High School Athletic Associations decries such attitudes and its members profess a belief that the high school athletic program must be confined within an educational framework. The Federation's beliefs are identified by its Executive Secretary as follows:

> First, we believe that the nature of a nation's sports program reflects, to a large degree, the nation's physical well-being and its physical interests. . . .
>
> Second, we believe in competition. It is beneficial for the highly skilled to compete, for the less skilled to compete, for the moderately skilled to compete. A desire to win is good, and most benefits occur when extreme effort is made; casual effort does not result in desirable benefits! We believe that there is a difference between recreational sports and competitive sports. And we believe further that competition should be regulated by standards.
>
> Third, we believe that we should win according to the rules and that ethical practices should not be abused or voided in order to win. A program that is properly administered, even though it is competitive, will give the educational benefits we are striving for.

Fourth, we believe that a program with both breadth and depth is needed. There should be a great many sports opportunities for high school students and students should have a choice of the activity in which they want to participate. We believe that there is need for many teams on various levels. Not all students want to participate in programs that are highly competitive. Some students do not care about this kind of activity; some are not interested in making the sacrifices that are necessary if they are to excel.

Fifth, we believe that sportsmanship is taught and that the objectives we hope to attain can be reached only when sportsmanship is given a consideration. We believe that current approaches to sportsmanship are often "namby-pamby." Even with the fear of oversimplifying this important area, we suggest that there are three standards for sportsmanship. You can have acceptable sportsmanship generally if you will play the game according to the rules, both the spirit of the rules and the actual rules. If you win you do not gloat over it. If you lose you do not alibi. We believe that some "window dressing" is insincere in the sportsmanship area, that it is unnecessary. Furthermore, it contributes to a weakness or a fault of our competitive program. We think that it is artificial and we believe that sportsmanship is dependent upon sincerity.

Finally, we believe that personal and social values can be attained in sports competition but that these objectives are not automatic and, to a great degree, they depend upon leadership.[2]

In order to meet desirable standards of interscholastic programs at secondary school levels, it seems that *minimally* a coach's background should reflect a study of the growth and developmental patterns of students and the medical aspects of sports, as well as a basic knowledge of the sport he is coaching. In its concern for the student athlete, the State of Ohio Board of Education, in September 1970, passed the following resolution.[3]

RESOLUTION "A"

WHEREAS, this Board has adopted A Guide for the Development of a School
Activity Program, and

WHEREAS, said Guide provides in part that:
Student participation in interscholastic athletics is restricted to those enrolled in the seventh grade or above. Students in grades seven and eight should not be permitted to participate in

---

2. Clifford Fagan, "Values in Interscholastic Sports," in *Values in Sports, Report of a National Conference* (Washington: American Association for Health, Physical Education and Recreation, 1963), pp. 11-12.

3. "State Board of Education Resolution," *The Ohio High School Athlete,* **30** (February 1971), p. 123. Reprinted with permission.

interscholastic athletics except when a broad and comprehensive program in physical education and intramurals exists for all boys and girls. The number of contests and types of sports, in which individual students participate, shall be kept at a minimum. Every control needed to insure the health, safety and physical well-being of the participant in interscholastic athletics shall be provided.

and

WHEREAS, the health and safety of students participating in interscholastic athletics continues to be a vital concern of this Board,

NOW THEREFORE BE IT RESOLVED that the following addition be made to said Guide:

The faculty member (coach) responsible for students participating in interscholastic athletics such as football, basketball, track and field, baseball and wrestling should evidence knowledge about the medical aspects of sports activities, and should continuously be apprised of the latest developments emanating from the medical and training research on sports activities.

and

BE IT FURTHER RESOLVED that the Superintendent of Public Instruction be, and hereby is, directed to distribute this addition to the Guide to all Superintendents and principals in the state, and to encourage and assist local school districts, the OHSAA and other education-related associations or agencies in planning and holding workshops or seminars for the purpose of developing appropriate knowledge and providing information on the latest developments in this field.

CURRENT TRENDS

Sports form one of the genuine bonds which help bring people together. Cozens and Stumpf acknowledge this concept:

Within a few decades, sports and games have spread over the whole world, leaping barriers of race, religion, and social class. The language of sport is

Field hockey, a popular interscholastic sport for girls. Photo courtesy of Ohio▶ Association for Health, Physical Education and Recreation.

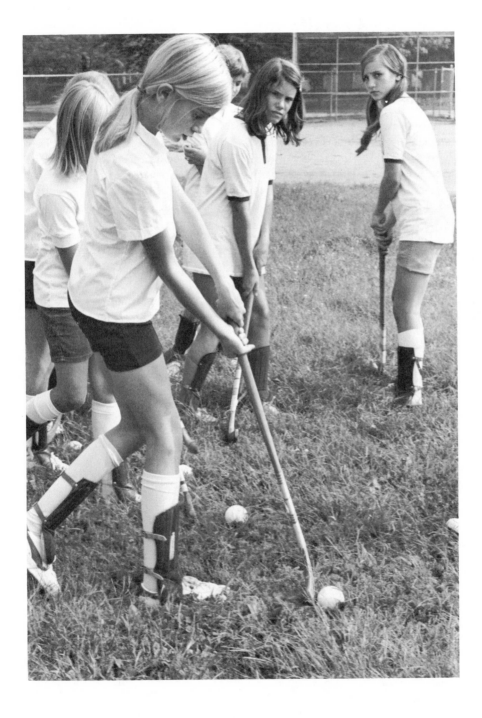

truly universal, and in the sportsman's code there is neither east nor west, neither white nor black, neither exploiter nor exploited.[4]

Although there is not universal agreement with this statement, particularly with the last phrase, there can be no denial of the fact that the growth of interschool athletic programs in the United States has been nothing short of spectacular. Statistics released by the National Federation of State High School Athletic Associations in 1969 reveal that 112,407 schools sponsored interschool competition in 29 sports, in which 3,456,350 students participated. Far from being restricted to the four activities historically associated with this type of program (football, basketball, baseball, and track and field), the list now includes such diverse sports as water polo, gymnastics, bowling, curling, volleyball, lacrosse, and riflery.

The phenomenal growth of interschool athletic programs for girls is not apparent in the figures above. However, as sociocultural concepts regarding female athletic prowess and femininity have changed, and as research has repudiated what were considered undesirable physiological and psychological effects of competition on girls and women, the opportunities for girls to compete have increased perhaps even more dramatically than for boys.

The fact that agencies sponsoring competitive athletic programs are not limited to educational institutions presents some distinctive problems, not the least of which are questions of standards and leadership. However, there seems to be genuine concern among the various sponsoring agencies about improving programs for the welfare of all participants, so one can be optimistic about the effects of competition.

Problems germane to Olympic competition must be solved and the age-old question of amateurism answered. Reasonable men, truly interested in sport and its congruent values and diligent in their attack on such problems, should be able to provide workable, equitable solutions.

The problems connected with interschool athletic competition, especially at the high school level, are quite varied, and efforts to solve them must consist of more than mere discussion. A solution that seems to promise the greatest likelihood of success in overcoming questionable athletic practices is the trend toward required certification of all coaches. To be certified, a coach must have more than a teaching degree. He must have taken courses covering the medical aspects of sports and the psychological and sociological foundations of coaching, and he must have become thoroughly grounded in specific game skills.

Curricula which prepare trainers and athletic administrators are also being introduced into American colleges. Since many sports are inherently dangerous,

4. Frederick W. Cozens and Florence Stumpf, *Sports in American Life* (Chicago: University of Chicago Press, 1953), p. 3.

it would be well to have qualified medical personnel at all games and practice sessions, but this is obviously an impossibility. Greater attention is therefore being paid to the qualifications of trainers, and courses are being prescribed which should enable them to handle most injuries competently.

The area of administration in athletics is no longer just a haphazard arrangement of "promoting" a faithful coach or "kicking upstairs" an unsuccessful one. A recent study in this area points out that most athletic administrators consider a master's degree essential and that courses included in such a degree should cover, in addition to physical education, such things as the science and philosophy of administration, accounting, public relations, management, psychology, and public speaking.[5] Since it is universally accepted that the quality of leadership determines the quality of the program, specific preparation for athletic administrators cannot help being efficacious.

Problems at the intercollegiate level are even more complex and more numerous. Basically, however, they are merely magnifications of problems at the high school level, and since most prospective physical educator-coaches will not commence their careers at the college level, we will give no special attention to these problems here. Those interested will find a cogent treatment of the entire spectrum of intercollegiate athletics in the recently published *Administration of Athletics in Colleges and Universities.*[6]

Like all other educational endeavors, the interschool athletic program is experiencing a new kind of problem as a new generation of student athletes enters the picture. Most boys and girls still have an interest in sports as well as a desire to participate in them; however, many will no longer accept what they consider infringements on their freedom in order to be members of varsity squads. Such things as length of hair, extremely restrictive training rules and regulations, and unquestioning attitude seem immaterial to many present-day athletes in their pursuit of athletic excellence. Consequently, if faced by the archetypal coach who refuses to change his procedures, many potentially good athletes simply drop out of the program, preferring instead to be true to their own convictions. It seems that a required background for all coaches in the behavioral sciences would help to alleviate this situation.

There are many other problem areas in athletics, and there are just as many proposed solutions to them. Not the least of the problems is of course financing.

---

5. Fredric W. Schuett, *A Comparison of Recommended Duties and Preparations of College Athletic Directors with Present Practices,* unpublished master's thesis, Kent State University, 1968.

6. National Association of College Directors of Athletics and Division of Men's Athletics, American Association for Health, Physical Education and Recreation, Edward S. Stietz (ed.), *Administration of Athletics in Colleges and Universities* (Washington: National Education Association, 1971).

Theoretically, if a program of athletics is educational, it ought to be financed as are other educational endeavors; that is, it should be completely subsidized by boards of education. Although this goal seems unattainable under the present tax structure for supporting public schools, it is worth fighting for, and we can hope that all educators will join in the struggle to guarantee such subsidy for all co-curricular programs.

SUMMARY

Play is man's heritage and as such is universally accepted; yet a long established resistance to organized programs of competitive athletics is also a heritage.[7] Adjustment of such diverse viewpoints depends on the efforts of reasonable, principled men and women to define acceptable and justifiable goals for interschool athletic programs, work untiringly to achieve them, and refuse to yield to pressures which would destroy them. Oberteuffer[8] cites reasons for alarm about the future of athletic programs, and he states that it will take an organized effort to "stem the tide of anti-morality and anti-intellectualism" presently engulfing school athletics. It is hoped that some of the points brought out in this chapter will motivate all those interested in physical education and athletics to explore intelligently and scientifically the contributions which sports can make to the education of all boys and girls and then to develop programs which will ensure such contributions.

---

7. Edward J. Shea and Elton E. Wieman, *Administrative Policies for Intercollegiate Athletics* (Springfield, Ill.: Charles C. Thomas, 1967), p. 3.

8. Delbert Oberteuffer, "On Learning Values Through Sport," *Quest,* 1 (December 1963), pp. 23-29.

STUDENT PROJECTS

1. Survey the schools in the immediate area to determine the following:

   a) How many elementary schools sponsor interschool competition? In what sports? How many junior high schools?

   b) Are such programs conducted for both boys and girls?

   c) At the senior high school level: (1) How many sports are there in the interschool program? (2) How are they financed? How many activities are self-supporting? Which ones? (3) Compare the program for girls to the program for boys.

2. Interview coaches to determine what they consider the greatest problems in interscholastic athletics.

3. How is the girls' intercollegiate athletic program at your university financed? If financed differently than the boys' program, why?

4. Compare the responsibilities of the Division for Girls' and Women's Sports with those of the National Collegiate Athletic Association or the National Federation of High School Athletic Associations.

5. Interview professors representative of a cross-section of disciplines to get their reactions to the value of intercollegiate athletic programs.

6. How does the conduct of interschool athletic programs in the United States differ from that of the same type of program in selected foreign countries?

GLOSSARY OF TERMS

Athletics That part of the total physical education program which centers around interschool or intercollegiate sports participation.

Varsity A highly select group of players who receive extra coaching and who participate in prescheduled athletic contests.

State High School Athletic Association That body in a particular state to whom the State Board of Education delegates the responsibility for the conduct of interscholastic athletic programs.

Intramurals A program of recreational activities carried on within the school. These activities may or may not be competitive and may or may not be athletic.

Extramurals The extension of the intramural program to include more than one school. For example, all intramural winners from one school may compete against the winners from another school.

Sports days A program of competition in one or more activities in which two or more schools are involved and school identity is maintained.

Play day A program similar to a sports day, except that school identity is *not* maintained. Competing teams are selected from representatives of all participating schools.

SELECTED REFERENCES

1. Boyle, Robert H. *Sport—Mirror of American Life.* Boston: Little, Brown, 1963.
2. Coutts, Curtis A. "Freedom in Sport." *Quest,* **10** (May 1968), pp. 68-71.
3. Division for Girls' and Women's Sports and Division of Men's Athletics. *Values in Sports.* Washington: American Association for Health, Physical Education and Recreation, National Education Association, 1963.
4. Educational Policies Commission, National Education Association. *School Athletics.* Washington: National Education Association, 1954.
5. Hein, Fred V. "Why Some Boys Should Stay Off the Team," *Today's Health* (August 1967), pp. 71-72.
6. Loy, John W. "The Nature of Sport: A Definitional Effort." *Quest,* **10** (May 1968), pp. 1-15.
7. McIntosh, Peter C. *Sport in Society.* London: C. A. Watts, 1963.
8. National Association of College Directors of Athletics and Division of Men's Athletics, American Association for Health, Physical Education and Recreation. Edward S. Stietz, ed. *Administration of Athletics in Colleges and Universities.* Washington: National Education Association, 1971.
9. Resick, Matthew C., Beverly L. Seidel, and James Mason. *Modern Administrative Practices in Physical Education and Athletics.* Reading, Mass.: Addison-Wesley, 1970.
10. Sanborn, Marion, and Betty Hartman. *Issues in Physical Education.* Philadelphia: Lea and Febiger, 1970.
11. Savage, Howard J. *American College Athletics,* Bulletin 23. New York: Carnegie Foundation for the Advancement of Teaching, 1929.
12. Scott, Harry A. *Competitive Sports in Schools and Colleges.* New York: Harper, 1951.
13. Scott, Jack. *Athletics for Athletes.* Hayward, Calif.: Quality Printing Service, 1969.
14. Shea, Edward J., and Elton E. Wieman. *Administrative Policies for Intercollegiate Athletics.* Springfield, Ill.: Charles C. Thomas, 1967.
15. Shecter, Leonard. *The Jocks.* Indianapolis: Bobbs-Merrill, 1969.
16. Sheehan, Thomas J. "Sport: The Focal Point of Physical Education," *Quest,* **10** (May 1968), pp. 59-67.
17. Stoke, Harold W. "College Athletics, Education or Show Business?" *Atlantic Monthly* (March 1954), pp. 46-50.
18. Stone, Gregory P. "American Sports: Play and Displays" *Chicago Review,* **9** (Fall 1955), pp. 83-100.

relationship of physical education to recreation

chapter 11

To be able to fill leisure intelligently is the last product of civilization.

BERTRAND RUSSELL

Recreation has only recently taken its place among the professions. It has become a profession in part because of the needs of an increasing world population: a decrease in free recreative space, an increase in nonworking hours, and an increase in life expectancy for the general population.

Formerly the various branches of recreation were taught and administered within other areas of specialization. Physical and sports activities were taught by physical educators, nature study by conservationists, and painting by artists. Little or no coordination existed between the different groups who were serving the recreational needs of people. Municipal recreation seemed to have very little in common with park management. Fortunately, that lack of coordination has largely disappeared. Rapid means of transportation now bring the city recreation program to the parks. The city, which controls the water systems for use as designated by the water department, is at times forced to open lakes and reservoirs for recreational uses. The administration of these water activities may be entrusted to the city's recreation department.

As needs for recreation specialists increased, colleges and universities began to offer preparatory courses in recreation leadership. Because the personnel involved were lacking in expertise, such programs were often multidisciplinary. The multidisciplinary pattern was thus a product of necessity, but it proved to be a strong advantage because it drew on the talents found in the related fields of biology, geology, physical education, and astronomy—to name just a few.

Later divergent groups, such as park managers, city recreation directors, industrial recreation directors, and others began to hold joint meetings to form professional associations. Strength of purpose, program, and personnel followed. Recreation no longer needs to depend on other fields to train its personnel although it will always continue to call on the expertise available in selected areas of preparation.

The fact that even professional educators tend to think of the fields of physical education and recreation as synonymous contributes to the confusion of terminology discussed in Chapter 1. A similar problem is that recreation is at times interpreted to mean solely "play," leisure time, or physical activity. Although each one of these interpretations is correct in some degree, none suffices as a definition of recreation as a field of study or discipline.

There are a number of definitions of play and various theories on why animals, including humans, play. Some of the theories propose, for example, that children play because they have surplus energy, that they are reliving in play the history of the human race, that they instinctively know what they will do in later life, that the basic drive to play is similar to the drive to seek food, that children play because of their social contacts with others. There seems to be some foundation to each theory, and yet no one is adequate by itself, and most of them are unable to explain the play patterns of large segments of the human race.

Since play may be considered part of recreation, it may have some of the characteristics of recreation, but no definition of play is completely satisfying as a definition of recreation. The same limitation applies to leisure, which can be defined as "the unobligated hours available after caring for employment or the activities mandatory for self-maintenance."[1] Again, leisure time is part of the recreation whole, not synonymous with it. Carlson, Deppe, and McClean defined recreation as "any enjoyable leisure experience in which the participant voluntarily engages and from which he receives immediate satisfaction."[2] Most writers on recreation prefer to define it in terms of the characteristics which mark recreative activities.

THE CHARACTERISTICS OF RECREATION

Recreation encompasses many activities, from those of a quiet, sedentary type to vigorous contact sports. This fact influences the philosophers among the recreation specialists to shy away from a short and concise definition of the discipline and to favor one that combines a number of descriptive characteristics.

> Recognizing that the task of the recreation professional is a varied and complex one, and that he may appear in many different lights to different observers, it is appropriate at this point to examine the meaning of the term "recreation" itself. Most people—including many professionals in this field—feel they have a fairly good idea of what this is. But, when they are pinned down and asked to define the word, the results are likely to be contradictory and confused.[3]

When one peruses the literature in the recreation field, the similarities in the descriptions of the *characteristics* of recreation become very pronounced. Among those most often listed are the following characteristics.

1. A recreational activity must be voluntary. As soon as a person is forced into an activity by pressure of individuals or peer groups, it is no longer considered recreational in nature.

2. To be recreational, an activity must take place during leisure time. The fact that one enjoys his occupation does not make it recreational. Occasionally, however, skill in a recreational activity may lead to an occupation, such as art or professional sport.

---

1. Reynold E. Carlson, Theodore R. Deppe, and Janet R. McClean, *Recreation in American Life,* (Belmont, Calif.: Wadsworth, 1963), p. 6.

2. *Ibid.,* p. 7.

3. From *Recreation Today: Program Planning and Leadership,* by Richard Kraus. Copyright © 1966 by Meredith Publishing Company, p. 5. Reprinted by permission of Appleton-Century-Crofts, Educational Division, Meredith Corporation.

3. There must in fact be activity, not mere passive diversion. Daydreaming, taking a nap, and sitting on a park bench may be restful, but they are not recreative in nature, as are such quiet activities as bridge and painting.

4. To be recreational, an activity must be intrinsically enjoyable. Since it is voluntary and takes place during free time, no one should participate in an activity he doesn't enjoy. Recreational activities are not performed for social acceptance or reward.

5. To be recreational, an activity must have social acceptance. Stealing hub caps might well fulfill some of the criteria, but the practice is not accepted by society in general.

6. To be recreational, an activity must provide a change from one's usual activity. A professional painter cannot paint "for recreation" within the definition of that term, although he may indeed enjoy painting (see 2 above). Neither would a professional golfer playing nontournament golf be considered to be participating in recreational activity.

7. To be recreational, an activity must not be related to personal or family maintenance. Eating, grooming, and housekeeping are thus excluded as recreational activities except under circumstances limited enough to be insignificant.

8. To be recreational, an activity must permit creative responses. Although regimentation may be necessary in some recreational activities, it must not be of a degree to stifle creative individual responses to the problems presented in the activities.

THE NEED FOR RECREATION

From the earliest of primitive times, man hunted and fished for food to survive, and in such pursuits he protected himself from attack. Yet even in those times, he amused himself with objects of play. Furthermore, when it was no longer necessary that he hunt and fish for survival, he did so for the pleasure he found in the activity, and hence recreation was born. The history of recreation activities parallels that of physical education, as described in Chapter 2, and it is sometimes impossible to separate the two. Recreation has always been needed, but the reasons for the needs have varied throughout history. A review of the needs, especially those of the present day, seems to be in order.

1. The Expansion of Leisure. Except for members of the ruling classes in Western Europe, the expansion of leisure occurred only after the invention of industrial machines. In the early days of the Industrial Revolution, some machines produced more goods but actually increased the length of the working day.

The Greeks, on the other hand, had taken time for their recreative pursuits, and so had the Romans. During the time of Nero, the Romans were reported to have 159 holidays that were devoted to spectacles. Unfortunately, most of the Romans were merely spectators, and the slaves in combat could hardly be considered as engaging in recreation!

The period after World War I marked the beginning of the reduction of the work week. After the Great Depression the work week was further reduced, either because of the economics of supply and demand or because of legislation enacted to bring the crisis to a solution. During that period the rise of a united labor force was the greatest single factor in effecting the reduction of the work week—a process that continues even today. A work week shorter than 40 hours is no longer a dream. The two-day weekend has long been a reality. In many occupations the midweek half-day break is common practice. This additional released time will make demands on recreation facilities. A recent suggestion that reservations be required before admission to our national parks is one way in which to cope with the hordes that descend on them at critical periods of the year.

Recreation programs must be planned to meet the increase in leisure in ways other than the sedentary pursuits of radio and television.

2. Rise of Urban Centers. When America was predominantly rural, the process of earning a living demanded long hours, but opportunities for recreation abounded. There were fish to catch, game to hunt, mountains to climb, and fresh streams to swim. Groups gathered together for such social occasions as plowing and husking bees, log tossing and rolling, and the combative sports of men. As time passed, however, buildings rose, the streets became hard, and man moved inward and upward. Land has become increasingly expensive and decreasingly available for leisure time play or recreation. In this setting, men run machines, mostly in a sedentary position. There is certainly a paradox in the fact that men work with machines for the better life, and yet they keep decreasing the space in which they can enjoy the fruits of their labors. Men need now to replace the opportunities for recreation in the setting they have created for themselves or to be transported away from it for their leisure.

3. The Changing Social Structure. In the past the family unit was the center of most recreation activities. Changes that have been evolving for many years are due to changes in life patterns, including the change from home-centered to business-centered employment. The commuting father placed the burden for family recreation on the mother. Because of the shortage of labor during World War II, the working mother also abrogated much of the responsibility. The trend still continues in this direction, and only time will tell what the present Women's

Liberation movement will bring. Some agency must then fill the void and provide leadership to the children in this setting.

Another social factor deserving consideration is the need of the aged for recreation. The time gap between either forced or voluntary retirement and death is increasing steadily. Retired persons who have worked hard all their lives to support themselves and rear their families seek pleasurable ways in which to spend their golden years. They are in need of adequate recreation. Meyer, Brightbill, and Sessoms have listed the needs of the aging in the following manner.[4]

1. The need to be considered as a real part of the community.
2. The need to occupy much expanded free time in more satisfactory ways.
3. The need to render some socially useful service.
4. The need to enjoy normal companionships.
5. The need for recognition as an individual.
6. The need to have opportunity for self-expression.
7. The need for a sense of achievement (is tied up with number 5).
8. The need to feel free to slow down on work or activities.
9. The need to have health protection and care.
10. The need for suitable mental stimulation.
11. The need for suitable living arrangements.
12. The need for wholesome family relationships.
13. The need for spiritual satisfaction.

THE VALUES OF RECREATION

When one discusses the values that accrue from participation in most disciplines or professions, the possibility of making unsubstantiated claims becomes real. Recreation does not profess to be a cure for juvenile delinquency or the salvation of the aged. It may contribute to both, however. Among the values associated with recreation in its many aspects are the following.

1. There are opportunities to develop physically through muscular activity. Some activities, such as handball and swimming, develop the cardiovascular system, some develop strength, and others help develop coordination. The degree of contribution usually depends on the intensity of the activity and the time devoted to it.

---

4. Harold D. Meyer, Charles K. Brightbill, and H. Douglas Sessoms, *Community Recreation*, 4th ed. (Englewood Cliffs, N.J.: Prentice-Hall, 1969), pp. 337-338.

2. There are opportunities to enhance the educative process through recreational activities. Play permits children to investigate the immediate surroundings, and solutions are often determined by trial and error. Activities such as photography permit the participant to learn about the processes necessary for the development of pictures.

3. There are opportunities to discover innate creativity through exposure to the fine arts. Activities such as painting, music, dramatics, and gymnastics permit the participants to express themselves in their relationships with their world.

4. There are opportunities to engage in and improve social interaction in acceptable situations. Camping presents many opportunities for people of different states and different countries to get to know one another in an informal and friendly atmosphere. Bowling and golf leagues permit people of all ages to unite for a common goal. For young children, the opportunity of learning to compete under socially acceptable conditions is essential. The sacrifices one must make for the common good and the cooperation necessary for success can be imparted through these activities.

5. There are opportunities for a change in pace from one's everyday life. No matter how enjoyable one's work is, there is a need to get away from it occasionally. Even when a person makes a living doing what he enjoys most, he derives benefits from detaching himself from it. Painters who love to paint and professional golfers or baseball players certainly do have enjoyable vocations, and yet in the late stages of a long season, they need a change. There are enough forms of recreation to satisfy the needs of most people for change.

6. There are opportunities for individuals to obtain the satisfaction and pleasure of a personal achievement. The unbounded enjoyment of leisure time might be the greatest value of them all. A person can set his own goal. A mountain climbed, a trout caught, a tent pitched, or a ball struck can be sheer joy to one who has never had such an experience. To another such joy may come from a first sketch in a drawing class or a simple finesse in bridge. That is what recreation is all about.

HOW RECREATION IS ORGANIZED AND ADMINISTERED
TO MEET NEEDS AND VALUES

Since recreation activities range widely—for example, from mountain climbing to collecting sea shells—there is no one organizational pattern which can suffice for all types of recreation available in the United States today. The following paragraphs explain briefly the administrative responsibilities of the principal areas of recreation.

Community Recreation Department. A recreation department that is an arm of the formal community government gets its financial support from tax sources, general funds, or funds raised by special levies. It may or may not be connected with the school system. Since it gets its money directly from the people, the department does not ordinarily compete for the dollar with other units. It provides low-cost recreation for all of the citizens of the community by utilizing existing buildings and outdoor areas. The necessity of maintaining separate staffs and facilities may be considered a disadvantage.

School-centered Recreation. When community recreation is centered in the local school system, the existing facilities are more readily available. Utilization time of school buildings is increased. There is also a ready staff available to man the facilities. In this situation, however, recreation is competing with the school for money. Whenever a conflict of schedules develops, it is usually the recreation program that is altered. Furthermore, participants may feel that recreation in a sense becomes an extension of the school day—to the detriment of a real feeling of recreation.

School and Community Recreation. A combined organization offers the advantages of both of the separated systems, especially in the small to medium-sized communities that cannot afford separate sets of facilities. In some larger cities (for example, Cleveland, Ohio) it also works very well.

State and Federal Governments. Through their systems of forests and parks, both the state and federal governments provide a wide range of recreation activities as part of their services. Camping, hunting, fishing, hiking, horseback riding, swimming, and golf, which are included in such programs, are usually low-cost activities. Since the available park lands and forests remain fixed in extent, the existing facilities are now becoming overcrowded. Areas once considered remote are now readily accessible by modern means of transportation.

City Government. In addition to specifically including recreation departments within their structures, many cities provide related facilities for recreation purposes. Libraries, zoos, concert halls, and theaters expand a city's recreation possibilities. Some subdivisions within the city are planning recreation services during the development of the area along with such standard items as sewers, sidewalks, and roads.

Industrial Recreation. Most large, modern business organizations now provide recreation programs for their staffs and employees. World War II programs proved so successful in both improving employee morale and increasing production that recreation leaders are now considered indispensable members of business firms. Programs are limited only by the imagination of those in charge. Music groups, theater, athletic teams, and craft classes are found in many such programs.

Geriatric Centers. Among the more interesting recent developments in the recreation field is the provision of recreation for senior citizens. Most of these people are retired, and they are seeking worthwhile recreation activities. States such as Florida, California, and Arizona have been particularly concerned with this area of recreation because large numbers of older citizens have moved to those states. Retirement villages have sprung up where retired persons enjoy common interests.

Commercial Recreation. During periods of affluence, commercial recreation facilities are constructed at a very rapid rate. Golf courses, bowling alleys, tennis clubs, ski resorts, archery ranges, and trampoline areas are examples. Adding these new facilities to the older fishing and hunting camps and seaside resorts, one can see the impact of recreation activities. Though often criticized by the recreation professional, these resorts must be good to survive. Programs must be well conducted and interesting.

Fraternal Organizations and Service Clubs. The American Legion has sponsored a youth baseball program for many years. The Fraternal Order of Police sponsors the PAL program, which provides organized activities for needy youngsters. Little need be said for the long-standing programs of both the YMCA and the YWCA; indeed, in historical terms, it is difficult to separate physical education in the United States and the development of the YMCA movement.

THE PHYSICAL EDUCATOR AND RECREATION

Although presently the disciplines of physical education and recreation have a great deal of autonomy, at one time the source of personnel for recreation was primarily the physical education schools. Recreation became an avocation or even the second occupation of the physical educator. During this period, most recreational activities were mainly physical in nature. With the extension of recreation to include a wide variety of activities and the development of a separate philosophy, the profession of recreation began to develop its own personnel with specialties in community recreation, industrial recreation, recreational therapy, and park management. The curricula at a number of institutions reflected this change at both the undergraduate and graduate levels. Recreation has come into its own as a profession. The physical educator still has his place in recreation, but he is usually a specialist in playground direction, much as the art instructor is a specialist in, say, painting.

Since many high school students do not go on to higher education, the physical education program should include some of the activities which the student can use throughout adult life. The Lifetime Sports Education Project has been instrumental in having such sports as tennis, golf, bowling, trap-shooting, archery, and bait and fly casting added to the curriculum in many schools throughout the country. This goal has been achieved mainly by offering a series of workshops and clinics to teachers in various parts of the country. Most have been conducted by well-known experts in the particular sports and sponsored jointly by the Lifetime Sports Education Project and the state or national professional organizations.

The job opportunities in recreation are excellent. There will be a shortage of personnel in the foreseeable future. Most of the areas mentioned in the preceding section on administration are shorthanded. In addition, the colleges and universities that offer courses in recreation are in need of key personnel. As the general population increases, continued periods of prosperity and a general increase in leisure will continue to compound the situation.

STUDENT PROJECTS

1. Visit in a group and/or research the different types of recreation programs (municipal, industrial, private, etc.) and report your findings to the class.

2. Investigate the occupational opportunities in the recreation field.

GLOSSARY OF TERMS

Leisure "The unobligated hours available after caring for employment or the activities mandatory for self-maintenance." (Carlson, Deppe, and McClean)

Recreation "Any enjoyable leisure experience in which the participant voluntarily engages and from which he receives immediate satisfactions." (Carlson, Deppe, and McClean)

Play Voluntary participation in a game or activity, either educational or recreational in nature.

SELECTED REFERENCES

1. Brantley, Herbert, and H. Douglas Sessoms (eds.). *Recreation Issues and Perspectives.* Columbia, S.C.: Wing, 1969, pp. 111-167.

2. Carlson, Reynold E., Theodore R. Deppe, and Janet R. McClean. *Recreation in American Life.* Belmont, Calif.: Wadsworth, 1963.

3. Danford, Howard G. *Creative Leadership in Recreation.* Boston: Allyn and Bacon, 1964.

4. Kleindienst, Viola, and Arthur Weston. *Intramural and Recreation Programs for Schools and Colleges.* New York: Appleton-Century-Crofts, 1964.

5. Kraus, Richard. *Recreation Today: Program Planning and Leadership.* New York: Appleton-Century-Crofts, 1966.

6. Meyer, Harold D., Charles K. Brightbill, and H. Douglas Sessoms. *Community Recreation,* 4th ed. Englewood Cliffs, N.J.: Prentice-Hall, 1969.

7. Nash, Jay B. *Philosophy of Recreation and Leisure.* Dubuque, Iowa: Wm. C. Brown, 1960.

8. _____. *Recreation: Pertinent Readings.* Dubuque, Iowa: Wm. C. Brown, 1965.

9. _____. *The Organization and Administration of Playgrounds and Recreation.* New York: A. S. Barnes, 1936.

10. Neumeyer, Martin H., and Esther S. Neumeyer. *Leisure and Recreation.* New York: A. S. Barnes, 1936.

∟

relationships of physical education with health education as a profession

chapter 12

It is better to lose health like a spendthrift than to waste it like a miser.

BALZAC

"Health and physical education" have been used as one term so long in different settings of education that it is difficult to identify them as separate and distinct disciplines. Many states still certify teachers of "health and physical education," and departments within the school structure are frequently so titled. It seems appropriate to examine the reasons for both the earlier pattern of combination and the growing tendency to separate the two into distinct disciplines.

A SHORT HISTORY OF HEALTH EDUCATION

Although health and the effects on it of the environment figured in writings in Colonial America, the subject was not dealt with as a separate entity in the schools of that period. William A. Alcott (1798-1859) is considered the father of school health education because he wrote on the school environment and necessary health services. Even in his day, however, health was linked to physical education, as the writings of Horace Mann indicate. As a result of Alcott's efforts, Massachusetts became the first state to require by law the teaching of health (1850). Harvard College had initiated a course in hygiene by 1818.

During the latter stages of the nineteenth century, the "marriage" of health and physical education became almost complete, probably because: (1) heads of departments of physical education were mostly medical doctors, (2) the objectives had much in common, and (3) the curricular needs of both were met, to a great extent, in common courses.

This union continued well into the twentieth century, although Thomas Wood and others were disturbed by the lack of attention devoted to health education. There were organizations promoting health education, including some within the federal government, but health continued to play a secondary role in departments of health and physical education and in professional associations. Meanwhile, health *services* were fully accepted and played a major role in the school.

Until after World War I, no teacher training institution offered a major in health education. The first major program was established in Teachers College, Columbia University, in the year 1920-1921. World War II became the real turning point, however. Because of the exploding knowledge in health education and the pressures from health-allied organizations, a number of institutions began offering separate degrees in health education, including master's and doctor's degrees.

A trend noted in the early 1970's is to distinguish the fields of health education and physical education through separate certification requirements. The day of the joint major at either the undergraduate or the graduate level has come to an end. Although the two fields still have some common objectives, they will no longer have common facilities or personnel. The discipline of health education has come of age. The effects of the separation on either of the two related fields is a matter of conjecture at this time. In an age of exploding knowledge and specialization, one can hope that both will benefit, but with growing difficulties in the tax support of public schools, both may suffer.

DEFINITION AND PURPOSES OF SCHOOL HEALTH EDUCATION

Health is that quality of life which permits an individual to function at his best within his environment. It has physical, mental, and social implications, which differ in individuals and groups. The necessary level of social and mental health of a student living in a residence hall may have little relevance for a hermit. In a similar sense, the level of physical health and fitness for a bank president is not the same as for a steel worker.

Although health education is ordinarily a joint venture of school and community, this chapter will concern school health education primarily and will refer to community health only when such reference is applicable. In maintaining this approach, we recognize nevertheless that the responsibilities for school health education may rest solely with the local health department or jointly with the schools and the local health department. For either organizational pattern, the purposes of the health education program should be the same.

1. To disseminate information to the student concerning health and those factors which have an impact on it. The information may range from the structure of the body to the use of community agencies for the solution of health problems.

2. To initiate a positive health attitude in the student. For example, the student may have adequate knowledge about the problems of smoking or weight control, but a change in attitude may be necessary before he will use that knowledge.

3. To influence the student to change his behavior now or in the future. In the final analysis, the test of health education is not what a person knows about the subject, but what he does about it.

It is often assumed that if a person acquires knowledge in a certain area, a change in his attitude and behavior in that area will naturally follow. Most of us are examples of the fallacy of this assumption. Indeed, the order may be reversed. A child may respond to a teacher's or mother's "brush your teeth" or "wash your hands" long before he understands dental caries or the germ theory of disease. Then, too, a student with excellent knowledge may be faced with a personal problem that causes an attitudinal change in him.

In order to achieve the three purposes cited above, health educators organize the health experiences of students into three categories: health instruction, school health services, and the school environment. All three make important contributions to the students' knowledge of health. They will be more fully discussed in the following sections of this chapter. The diagram in Fig. 12.1 shows how the three areas of health education can be arranged for administration in a joint school and community health department.[1]

HEALTH INSTRUCTION

Even though health, historically, was not a course in the academic sense of the word, some of what is considered health education was always taught in correlation with other subjects, as part of an integrated unit or project, or incidentally, during the great "teaching moments" which take place as a result of such happenings as tornadoes, hurricanes, earthquakes, or space landings. Under such circumstances, however, the great abundance of exploding health knowledge remained untaught, and serious gaps in health knowledge of students existed. Even with extensive planning, the teaching of health through a series of integrated projects or in correlation with subjects such as biology, physics, and social studies has been found wanting.

Every school needs a concentrated series of courses in health to deal with problems that confront students of different age and grade levels. Although some of these problems (such as acne) are of interest to only one grade or age level, many of the others cross many grade-level lines. The problem of drug abuse, for example, is beginning in the elementary schools and continuing throughout adult life.

The biggest problems confronting the schools are the selection of materials to be taught and the proper introduction and grade placement of such materials. Subjects which formerly were reserved for discussion at the upper secondary grades or college are now topics for study at the junior high school, and rightly so. Among them are the following.

1. Human Sexuality. Study begins in the early elementary grades with information about sex-role differences and continues throughout life. Early maturation and dating make the inclusion of proper materials at the junior high school level mandatory. The acceptance of pregnant girls in the total high school program and changes in the obscenity laws create a climate that underscores the need to continue the study of human sexuality.

---

1. Cyrus Mayshark and Leslie W. Irwin, *Health Education in Secondary Schools,* 2nd ed. (St. Louis: C. V. Mosby, 1968), p. 21.

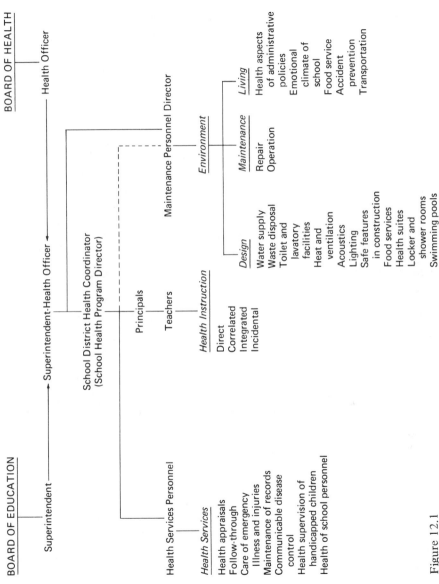

Figure 12.1

2. Drug Use and Abuse. Problems relating to drugs are no longer confined to the very few in the lower echelons of society or to the adult age group. Since cases of drug addiction are being discovered in children not yet in their teens, instruction on the dangers involved in drug use must begin at the elementary level before the students are subjected to the pressures of peers to adopt a life style that includes the use of drugs. Use of and traffic in glue sniffing, marijuana, LSD, and heroin have legal as well as social implications.

The effects of caffeine, alcohol, nicotine, amphetamine, and steroids were discussed in some detail in Chapter 8.

3. Environmental Problems. The pollution of the air we breathe and the water we drink has become a national emergency because it not only threatens our health but also constitutes aesthetic loss and diminishes recreation opportunities. The pollution of the nation's usable water may result in a severe water shortage in several decades unless the trend is reversed.

Radiation, in addition to polluting the air and water, accumulates in plants and animals, sometimes causing genetic changes in those forms of life. The effects of low-grade radiation are still virtually unknown. The dramatic effects of the "bomb" with its concussions, burns, and cancer-causing qualities are well established.

Pesticides, which were once proclaimed as saviors of mankind, are now suspected of causing a number of illnesses. Governmental agencies are urging caution and restraint in the use of most pesticides, and they have banned some entirely.

The use of food additives and substitutes has created hazards to the health of the user. Such additives and substitutes have been used to make food cheaper, more attractive, less fattening, and more appetizing. Some have been found to contribute to unhealthful conditions, especially as agents that may play a causative part in cancer, and they are now under study.

4. Mental Health. The promotion of good mental health and the avoidance of mental illness are dealt with at all grade levels in order to emphasize the preventive rather than the curative aspects of this growing problem. The manpower shortage attributable to mental health is among the nation's most critical, and it will not be easily solved. For this reason, early detection of minor problems and an emphasis on positive mental health are of crucial importance.

5. Social and Ethical Problems. The legal and ethical problems involved in organ transplants and in the control of the exploding population, for example, pose meaningful questions for both high school and college students. The very definitions of life and death are now being revised.

The topics suggested above, together with more traditional topics, such as rest, exercise, weight control, and consumer education, can make the contents of a relevant curriculum in health education from kindergarten through college vital and exciting. If such a course of study is to have meaning for the student, it must be taught from a psychological or problematical approach rather than from the exclusively physiological, or systems, approach that has been customary in the past. The development of concepts concerning health is more important than the accumulation of knowledge that rapidly becomes outdated.

SCHOOL HEALTH SERVICES

In addition to what the student is taught about health in the formal classroom, many of his experiences in and about the school add to his knowledge and attitudes about health. Since participation in health services is often very personal, a good program may be the principal tool in reaching a student. Although few public schools today can fully qualify, a good health service program should contain the following aspects.

1. Periodic Physical Examinations. Some states require an annual examination of all students attending elementary and secondary schools, but most do not. Where there is no such requirement, a periodic physical should be given four times during a student's schooling: (1) on first entering school, (2) during elementary school, (3) during junior high school, and (4) during senior high school.

At one time physical examinations were conducted on school premises, but at present the usual practice is for the family physician to examine the child and send the results to the school. The change to the physician's examining room should ensure a more thorough examination than could be provided in the school. Equipment is available for any special testing that may be necessary, and complete records are kept on the child's growth and development. Different arrangements, however, must be made for children of needy families.

2. Special Examinations. There are times other than the periods specified in the preceding paragraph when students will need to be seen by a physician. Athletes in contact sports and other vigorous activities, for example, should have examinations before being allowed to participate in athletics. The heart, lungs, teeth, and tonsils should be examined, and the student should be checked for hernia.

A special examination should also be given to a student after a prolonged absence from school because of illness to ensure his readiness to participate in physical education classes or athletics.

3. Examination Follow-up Program. One of the valid criticisms leveled at schools in the past has been the failure to use information gained from physical examinations. In the desire to adhere to the principle of "privileged communication," the results of examinations were "locked away" and seldom referred to. The school should make use of these records in any way that will benefit the student. A physical examination loses part of its value if there is no attempt to correct those deviations from the norm which are correctable. Parents or guardians must be informed about the health status of their children. If the parents cannot afford to have corrections made because of their financial status, referral to an agency that takes care of such matters is in order.

4. Vaccination and Inoculation Program. Although most states have compulsory vaccination and inoculation programs against communicable diseases as a school entrance requirement, schools in the states that do not must formulate their own requirements. The principal communicable diseases are virtually nonexistent in the United States, but they still abound in many parts of the world, and any relaxation of our program could lead to an epidemic. The immunization program in schools is occasionally objected to on the grounds of religious beliefs. Even when exceptions are made in such cases, the communicable diseases can be kept at a nonepidemic level in the student population unless unusual circumstances prevail. Among the diseases for which immunization should be required for school attendance are smallpox, diphtheria, whooping cough, poliomyelitis, tetanus, and measles. Standard immunizations for these diseases, with the possible exception of that for poliomyelitis, do not guarantee lifetime immunity and do require booster shots at specified intervals.

5. A System of Health Referrals and Health Consultations. Every school system should have a definite policy of dealing with students with health problems, including exclusion from class and exclusion from school. Minor illnesses may be handled by health service personnel, but recurrent or prolonged problems should be referred to the home or a community agency for solution. Exclusion from school sometimes involves legal problems, since the responsibility rests with the school that the student can reach home and that someone will be there when he arrives. The excluding officer of the school must be sure that these conditions are met before releasing an ill student. All teachers should recognize symptoms in health and behavior that might be significant and refer students exhibiting such symptoms to the health service or counselor. Sight and hearing problems, especially, often develop between the periodic health examinations.

6. First Aid and Safety Provisions. Most states have laws requiring each school building to provide a rest and recovery room for students. The room should contain cots, toilets, and lavatories. Since it is not feasible to have a doctor or even a nurse on duty at all times in each building, someone trained and certified in first aid should be readily available. Ideally, all teachers should be certified in first aid procedures.

A plan should be established for handling any type of emergency. The school should require each parent or guardian to complete a form containing pertinent information, including the name of the person to be notified in the event of an emergency. It should list the parent's name and phone number, family physician and phone number, and an alternative person to be notified when a parent cannot be reached, a person who has the legal right to make a decision regarding the child if he is sick or injured. A form of this type is shown in Figure 12.2. Such a form should be readily accessible and near a telephone.

EMERGENCY INFORMATION

1.	Student: Last name	First	Middle initial
	Parents or guardians: Last name	Father	Mother
	Address		Phone
	Parent's emergency number (employer):		Phone
2.	Family physician: Last name		First
	Address		Phone
3.	Other physician		
4.	In case of emergency, what hospital should be used?		
5.	Name of relative or friend who is approved to make decisions in case you cannot be reached.		Phone
6.	In case none of the above can be reached, may we have permission to make a decision?		

Yes   No

Signature

Figure 12.2

The information it contains must be kept current to be effective. Athletic coaches and intramural directors who stay after school with large numbers of students should have easy access to this information, or they should have their squad members complete similar forms for their own use.

7. System of Screening Tests and Observations. Since there may be three or four years between physical examinations, the school system should develop a series of screening procedures. Simple height and weight charts can bring to light deviations from the norm that occur between examinations and that can be investigated before they become serious. When combined with information on body typing, data on height and weight become extremely valuable.

Vision should be tested each year in the elementary grades. Either the Snellen or the Massachusetts Vision Test can be used. The latter is superior, though a little more costly, since it isolates conditions of farsightedness as well as nearsightedness. The classroom teacher can administer these tests with a minimum of training.

Hearing testing, in which audiometric devices are used, is much more sophisticated than vision testing and requires longer training periods for the tester. Ordinarily, the school speech and hearing therapist does this type of testing.

8. Health Supervision of School Personnel. Where state laws do not require that food handlers have medical examinations, the school board should do so. Since teachers, especially in the elementary schools, have very close contact with students, it should be mandatory that they be free of communicable disease. If nothing else, an annual certification of freedom from tuberculosis should be required. The trend in some states is toward annual examination of all teachers, paid for by the Board of Education. Some school boards will not release the first salary check until this condition is met. This type of plan is usually a local option of the Board of Education. The state of Maine, for one, requires that all teachers have an annual physical examination.

THE SCHOOL ENVIRONMENT

The location of the physical plant, the relationship of students to teachers, and the nature of the organization for instruction all have an impact on the health of the student. It is essential that the student be provided a most healthful school environment to enhance the learning process. A discussion on the effect of the environment on the student's health and the learning process follows.

1. The Physical Environment. A healthful school environment begins with the location of the school itself. It is difficult to change an established location, and therefore the initial selection of a school site affects students for decades. Is it near railroads, factories, or a main highway? Must most of the students cross the main part of the city to reach it? Is it located in the direction of the future growth of the city?

The disadvantages of old buildings located near noisy factories can be decreased by the use of tree screens between the noise and the school, by careful installation of acoustical tile, and by careful selection of courses to be taught on the noisy and quiet sides of the building.

The school environment also includes the color of the paint on the walls, lighting, humidity and heat, the condition of restrooms, and the adequacy of food services. Laboratories and workshops should be properly vented, and playfields, walks, and building approaches should be properly cared for.

Although most of these problems rest with the administration, an alert student body and teaching corps will ensure the maintenance of a healthful school environment. Because of their special expertise, health teachers and administrators have additional responsibility in these areas.

2. School Organization and Health. The manner in which the school day is organized and administered may have at least as much effect on the student as the physical makeup of the school. Among the factors to be considered are the following.

a) Length of the school day. It is estimated that the secondary school student now spends more than 1100 hours a year in school. There are advocates of a longer school day, but with the additional time spent on co-curricular work, most of the student's day is in fact spent in school. The school day is—and should be—gradually lengthened from kindergarten through senior high school, directly in proportion to the decrease in fatigue and the increase in attention span as the student grows older.

b) Length of class period. Similar to the problem of school day length is that of class period length. Fatigue and attention span must be considered, and shorter periods in the lower elementary grades permit frequent change in the types of activity. Such change is essential for a proper learning climate at that age level. Periods of 20-30 minutes are common at this level; periods of 40-45 are more usual in the junior and senior high school. At the college level the practice of dog-legging (double period on some days) is necessary to make efficient use of existing space when weekly meetings are variable.

c) Homework policy. Some schools have had to initiate a policy of limiting homework assignments to protect the students from demands for un-reasonable amounts of work by teachers who seem unaware of the requirements of other disciplines. The school may curtail homework by establishing a time limit per assignment or by restricting homework for each subject to specified days of the week. For instance, English, language, and mathematics teachers may be permitted to give homework on Monday, Wednesday, and Friday, whereas the science, humanities, and social studies teachers are restricted to Tuesday and Thursday.

d) *Curtailment of outside activities.* Often a student gets involved in too many extra- or co-curricular activities, either by choice or because he is forced by peer or parental pressure to participate. Some schools have restricted students to two or three extracurricular activities. Even though the activities sponsored by the school can be controlled, however, the student may still be subjected to a number of nonschool activities and lessons. The cumulative effect of school work, extracurricular activities, and private lessons may be detrimental to the student. When a student's mental and physical health are endangered by such excesses and pressures, the parents must be notified by the health or counseling services.

e. *Rewards for attendance.* A program of honoring students with perfect attendance records, though understandable in purpose, may actually perform a disservice to the teachers and student body. Some elementary school children come to school with communicable diseases in order to keep their records intact. The attendance certificate becomes of greater significance than their own health or the health of others they come in contact with. The practice of making awards for perfect attendance is fortunately dying out.

f) *Sick-leave program for teachers.* A similar threat to general health may stem from the school's sick-leave policy for teachers. If the teachers must pay for their own substitutes after a maximum number of absences, some will come to school with such communicable diseases as influenza, thus exposing students and other members of the faculty. On the other hand, a program which allows the accumulation of sick days for future use may result in a similar response: the teacher may "save" them for a protracted illness.

g) *Time placement of difficult subjects.* In the self-contained classroom of the elementary school, the teacher can arrange his course to meet the needs of the students. He can plan to teach his more difficult subjects during that part of the day when the students are most rested and relaxed, or he can alternate them with recreational types of classes, such as art, music, or physical education. Unfortunately, however, at most large secondary schools, not every student can have a desirable schedule. All subjects are taught during most hours of the school day, and the student must take them when they fit into the schedule and not when he is most fit to take them.

3. *The Teacher and Student Health.* The interpersonal relationships between the teacher and the students within the classroom have an impact on the health

of the students. Among the considerations which contribute to student health are the following.

a) *The make-up program following absence.* Frequently the procedures followed in having the student make up missed work are in direct contradiction to the practices of good health. Following an illness that necessitated absence from school, the student is often inundated with make-up work to complete while he is still recovering. In other words, immediately on his return to school, he is expected to produce more than the healthy student.

b) *Seating arrangements.* Because it is practical (administratively) to follow some ascending or descending alphabetical order in seating students, a teacher may inadvertently place students with sight or hearing problems in positions that may retard their progress in class. Taking attendance, collecting written work, and grading may be facilitated by this arrangement, but students may suffer for it. A proper health service identifies the students with handicaps tactfully and without the knowledge of the other students.

c) *Fear of the teacher or subject matter.* In a class where there is actual fear of physical harm for either poor performance or failure to perform at all, the student may suffer impairment of his health. If the teacher uses the technique of ridicule or embarrassment, the student may have a similar reaction. When exchanges between teachers and students occur in an atmosphere of mutual respect, stress and tensions are held to a minimum. Leniency in course requirements is not in any sense necessary to achieve this ideal, however. Students may learn to enjoy a difficult subject if they are encouraged whenever they show improvement and progress. Criticism of a student's actions may be offered in the interests of improvement, and creative self-expression is not stifled in a rush to conformity.

d) *Free expression.* Although the demand for student silence in a classroom may impair the learning process, the opposite may also be true. Young children forced to work in the bedlam that surrounds the overpermissive teacher may experience complete mental and physical fatigue at the end of the day. Studies have shown that excessive noise causes physical fatigue among factory workers, and one can reasonably assume the same effect on students.

e) *Overemphasis on one grade or performance.* There are situations in the educational system in which one performance may change the course of a student's educational life. An example is the series of scholarship examinations. Although such practices are common in Europe, no single test or performance should carry sufficient weight to cause extreme tension and frustration among the student body.

OCCUPATIONAL OPPORTUNITIES

The entire field of health sciences is rich in career opportunities which combine the excitement of exploding knowledge and a feeling of service to one's fellowman. At present and for the foreseeable future, there is a shortage of trained and qualified personnel in most areas of the health sciences, of which health education is a part. Furthermore, with the population increasing and with growing concern for the health needs of everyone, there will certainly be demands for more and more persons to become involved in health education as a career.

One thinks of health educators as being confined to formal educational systems, from the elementary schools to the universities. Far from it! Job opportunities exist in such voluntary health agencies as the American Cancer Society, the National Tuberculosis Association, and others. These organizations, which are supported by voluntary financial contributions and services, employ staff members at the national, state, and local levels. Since each agency is generally concerned with a specific health problem, trained personnel are hired to educate the public concerning that particular problem in an effort to combat or eradicate it.

There are also many opportunities in "official health agencies," the tax-supported arms of local, state, and federal government. Examples are city and county health departments, state health departments with their district offices, and the various divisions of the United States Department of Health, Education and Welfare (HEW). All employ health educators in various capacities in order to reach the public with their health messages.

Most of the state and national professional organizations employ health educators to make the public aware of certain health problems and their solutions. Professional associations are groups of individuals with a common background of service, a systematic curriculum and training, and some form of certification which legally allows them to practice their profession. Among the professional organizations employing health educators are the American Medical Association, the American Dental Association, and the American Association of Health, Physical Education and Recreation.

STUDENT PROJECTS

1. Poll a number of other students who are not members of this class to determine what types of health services were available to them in elementary and secondary school.

2. Report on the environmental factors in your present surroundings which have a direct impact on either the mental or the physical health of students.

GLOSSARY OF TERMS

Health That quality of life which permits an individual to function to an optimal degree within his environment.

School health education All the activities of the school and its environment which have an impact on the health of students and all other school personnel.

Health instruction Dissemination of health knowledge in order to develop concepts concerning specific health problems and to ensure good health practices.

Health services Those activities which appraise, conserve, and protect the health of the student.

Healthful school environment Physical and other conditions in the school which are conducive to the promotion of good health practices.

SELECTED REFERENCES

1. Anderson, C. L. *Community Health.* St. Louis: C. V. Mosby, 1969.
2. —————. *Health Principles and Practice.* St. Louis: C. V. Mosby, 1967.
3. —————. *School Health Practices,* 4th ed. St. Louis: C. V. Mosby, 1968.
4. Bucher, Charles A., Einar A. Olsen, and Carl E. Willgoose. *The Foundations of Health.* New York: Appleton-Century-Crofts (Meredith), 1967.
5. Byrd, Oliver E. *School Health Administration.* Philadelphia: W. B. Saunders, 1964.
6. Haag, Jessie Helen. *School Health Program,* rev. ed. New York: Holt, Rinehart and Winston, 1967.
7. Mayshark, Cyrus, and Leslie W. Irwin. *Health Education in Secondary Schools,* 2nd ed. St. Louis: C. V. Mosby, 1968.
8. Mayshark, Cyrus, and Donald Shaw. *Administration of School Health Programs.* St. Louis: C. V. Mosby, 1967.

9. Means, Richard K. *A History of Health Education in the United States.* Philadelphia: Lea and Febiger, 1963.

10. Nemir, Alma. *The School Health Program.* Philadelphia: W. B. Saunders, 1970.

11. Oberteuffer, Delbert, and Mary K. Beyrer. *School Health Education,* 4th ed. New York: Harper and Row, 1966.

12. Stiles, William W. *Individual and Community Health.* New York: McGraw-Hill, 1953.

13. Turner, C. E., Harriet B. Randall, and Sara Louise Smith. *School Health and Health Education,* 6th ed. St. Louis: C. V. Mosby, 1970.

responsibilities as a member of a profession

chapter 13

*In time a profession is like marriage, we cease to note
anything but its inconveniences.*

BALZAC

Teaching is one of the highest of all professions to which man can aspire. Because the term "profession" is misused to include many nonprofessional areas, it can be confusing. How does one distinguish between those positions which are professional and those which are not? What are the characteristics of a profession?

Characteristics of a profession

The nature of a profession differs from that of a trade, a business, or entertainment. The fact that one does or does not get paid for doing work has little to do with the professional nature of the work. One of the better lists of criteria of a profession, distributed as a memo by the Ohio Commission for Teacher Education, follows.

1. A profession involves activities essentially intellectual.
2. A profession commands a body of specialized knowledge.
3. A profession requires extended professional (as contrasted with solely general) preparation.
4. A profession demands continuous in-service growth.
5. A profession affords a life career and permanent membership.
6. A profession sets up its own standards.
7. A profession exalts service above personal gain.
8. A profession has a strong, closely knit, professional organization.
9. A profession enters into a convenant with its clientele.[1]

One does not become a member of a profession merely by signing a contract for money, as does the baseball or football professional athlete. One becomes a professional through a series of preparatory steps which are discussed in the following paragraphs.

A profession develops when there is a sufficient, unique body of knowledge to support its membership. This definition does not preclude the derivation of background information from other disciplines, but it does imply an accumulation of knowledge about one subject which is not common to other disciplines or professions.

A STUDENT MOVES TOWARD BECOMING A PROFESSIONAL

Teaching physical education involves the same type of commitment and involvement as does any other profession. Among the steps in becoming a professional are the following.

---

1. Ohio Commission on Teacher Education and Professional Standards, *TEPS and the Teaching Profession: A Position Statement and Concerns,* memorandum to local Teachers Associations, Columbus, May 22, 1969.

1. Selecting a University or College with a Good Course of Study in the Field of Choice. This first step involves those students who are attending junior colleges or two-year community colleges as well as those who are selecting a four-year institution. The course of study should involve general courses in the liberal arts, specific courses in education, and courses in the major field. No college or university can give the student experiences in all the physical activities he may be expected to teach or coach. Universities usually offer those most often taught in that particular locale. Additional skills are acquired at clinics, conventions, and in-service workshops. The new teacher is not expected to be an expert in all sports activities. The ability to teach and analyze is much more important.

Deficiencies in the physical-activities background of prospective teachers can be removed, but the time spent in this removal could better be spent in other facets of professional preparation. In addition, if the university or college has a high set of professional standards, that fact increases the possibilities for employment and acceptance for future graduate studies.

2. Beginning a Professional Library. The major student should begin his personal, professional library with his first courses in school. Unlike the lawyer and the doctor, whose initial libraries may be an expensive venture, the professional physical educator may acquire an adequate library at modest cost. Nevertheless, he may become the resource person in the community on activity buildings and the dimensions of playing areas for sports. Books from early courses serve as reference materials for later ones. Books should be supplemented by professional journals as soon as possible to ensure a source of current research and literature.

In addition to beginning his own personal library, the preprofessional student must learn to use the research facilities afforded to him in modern college and university libraries. The interlibrary loan policy opens up unlimited resources to him. Proper use of the library is basic to his professional growth.

3. Joining Professional Student Major Clubs. Most teacher education institutions have professional and sports interest clubs. The former have the advantage of fostering professional growth among the members. Two national fraternities (Delta Psi Kappa for women, and Phi Epsilon Kappa for men) have chartered units on many campuses. Interest clubs give the students an opportunity to improve their skills in activities which may have limited exposure in the curriculum.

4. Joining Professional Organizations. Most of the state associations have special student membership dues, sections in periodicals, and student sections at conventions. Students elect their own officers and are represented on the representative assembly or its equivalent.

Recently the American Association for Health, Physical Education and Recreation announced the appointment of two staff consultants who are to assume the responsibilities of coordinating the student section and major club development. The district conventions of AAHPER and the national convention have placement services available to help the members, including students.

5. Attending Workshops and Clinics. Since the curriculum cannot include all the activities in various programs, and since many of those offered cannot be covered in depth, most universities, colleges, and sports associations offer a number of workshops, clinics, and institutes. Usually the speakers are nationally known educators, players, and coaches. The student may never again have access to so many talented professionals. Some workshops, especially those of several weeks' duration, carry academic credit.

6. Attaining the Highest Academic Achievement. Since there is no such thing as terminal education, and since most states certify the beginning teacher only provisionally, additional schooling beyond the baccalaureate degree will be necessary. It is advantageous to maintain grades above average in order to gain admission to graduate studies rather than continue work on the undergraduate level. The work taken toward permanent certification can then apply to an advanced degree. A good academic average ensures the student a choice of schools and levels he wishes to pursue.

CONTINUED PROFESSIONAL GROWTH

Any profession depends on its membership for the leadership that commands the respect of other fields of study. Such men as Sargent, Hetherington, Wood, Williams, Nash, and others have brought the profession up a long hard road. The present leadership has continued to follow the examples of these great men. The leadership of the future will be provided by the present group of students and young teachers who must prepare themselves for the future. Such preparation includes the following.

1. Membership in Professional Organizations. The American Association for Health, Physical Education and Recreation, the American College of Sports Medicine, the American School Health Association, the National Association of Physical Education for College Women, the National College Physical Education Association for Men, and the National Recreation and Park Association are among the organizations available to the professional physical educator. These organizations develop and disseminate new ideas in the field, offer consultative services to the membership, provide opportunities (through journals and meetings) for debating and discussing vital issues, and serve as a medium for employment information. Recently, the national organizations have become

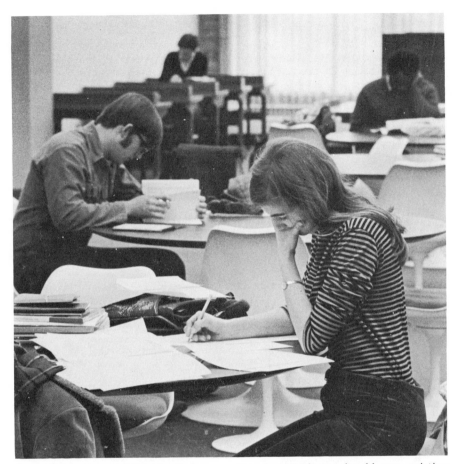

In addition to establishing their own libraries, students should use existing library facilities. Photo courtesy of Kent State University News Service.

more active politically in areas that concern their members. In order to upgrade the areas of health, physical education, and recreation, workers in those fields should join professional associations as most members of the legal or medical profession do.

2. Advanced Study. Work beyond the baccalaureate degree is required by most states for a life or permanent certificate. This work may be a continuation of meaningful undergraduate work or study toward an advanced degree. Since most school systems relate salary range to degree attainments, study beyond the baccalaureate is best spent working toward an advanced degree.

The teacher should exert the same care and planning in selecting a graduate school that he exercised in selecting an undergraduate school. Unfortunately, the choice of graduate schools may be limited by the teacher's performance at the undergraduate level. In a 1967 study, Resick found that 103 of 151 institutions required at least a C+ average for admission.[2] Other factors considered were a major or minor in the field, a specific average for the final two years, letters of recommendation, and a standard entrance examination. Some of the institutions surveyed accepted graduate students on probation when their qualifications were slightly below the acceptable standards. Thus there are strong reasons for the stress on good academic achievement at the undergraduate level.

3. Attendance at Conventions, Workshops, Clinics, and In-service Meetings. The athletic coaches in their specialities take this means to growth more seriously than do other teachers. Failing to keep up with new ideas in athletics helps to ensure an early professional demise. Teachers in the classroom, in the gymnasiums, or on the playing fields are not reviewed by the public every week, and they may tend to become complacent. That one belongs to a professional organization is not enough; new ideas come from reading the research and ideas expressed in the journals. New ideas also come from exchanges at conventions, including informal ones in the elevators and the lobbies of hotels. The authors consider a convention successful if it has uncovered one hot, usable idea, and the same criterion can be applied to a workshop or clinic. Better methods, newer approaches and a better insight into problems usually result from such attendance.[3] Conventions cover a variety of areas within a field. Clinics ordinarily cover one sport or activity. Workshops center on a specific area within a field of study. Finally, in-service meetings are based on the needs of the group. All have one goal in common—to upgrade the teachers in a school system or within a discipline.

4. Research and Writing. The life blood of any profession is its growth and development through philosophic concepts and ideas expressed in its professional journals and research reported in its research publications. A discipline exists only if it has a unique body of knowledge. Ideas may be lost if they are not recorded and disseminated to the membership. A profession that merely maintains the status quo stagnates.

New methods, new activities, means of evaluation and its effect on people—these are the results of research. Although no professional likes to be faced with the old threat of "publish or perish," many professionals need to be

2.   Matthew C. Resick, "Graduate Patterns," address presented at the Graduate Education Conference, Washington, January 8, 1967.
3.   Matthew C. Resick, "Let's Turn Pro." *The Physical Educator,* 17 (December, 1960), pp. 135-136.

prodded off "dead center." By demanding an investigation of what now exists, research in itself improves the individual. In describing the reasons for research, Steinhaus answered the question "Why this research?" by resort to analogy:

> Woodchopping produces both useful wood and a better woodchopper. Research must give to our fields the building materials of accurate facts and principles with which to construct sound practice and wise philosophy. It must supply ideas to kindle enthusiasm in our professional ranks and, in the public mind, a warm reception for our programs.[4]

5. *Excellence in Teaching.* The professional approaches each day, each class, and each assignment with the hope of doing the best possible job. Good teaching is the base of any teaching field. Every lesson should be evaluated as to its effect on the plans for the course. Every teacher's class receives an evaluation from the students as they leave. It may be a simple comment such as "a waste of time" or "enjoyable lesson" or "good class."

In some institutions rewards tend to be given mostly to those who are involved in research or writing, since these two facets of teaching are easy to measure. In the past several years a real effort has been made to identify those individuals who excel in the classroom and to give them monetary awards, plaques, or simply titles like "teacher of the year."

As the educator becomes more professional, he becomes aware of the broader aspects of his field and of all education.

> Each educator has a five-way concern in his educative efforts. By no priority but by a sequence of logic it might be stated that the first concern is for the *student.* The second concern is for the *subject matter.* The third concern is for the *profession of specialization.* The fourth concern is for the *total education enterprise,* and the fifth concern is toward *man in the world.* The good teacher may find only the first two ways to be concerned—for the student and for his own subject matter. The true professional concerns himself with the first, the second, the third, the fourth, and the fifth educational endeavors.[5]

RESPONSIBILITIES AS A PROFESSIONAL

In addition to performing his duties in a professional manner, the professional has several other responsibilities. By his work, research, speeches, and writing he contributes to the advancement of his profession.

---

4. Arthur H. Steinhaus, "Why This Research?" in M. G. Scott (ed.), *Research Methods,* 2nd ed. (Washington: American Association for Health, Physical Education and Recreation, 1959), p. 17.

5. Leona Holbrook, "Education is Our Business," *Journal of Health, Physical Education and Recreation,* 37 (April 1966), pp. 19, 81.

A true professional in physical education is interested and informed about the other disciplines within his school. He is knowledgeable in the area of philosophy of education being pursued within the school system and the contributions of his field toward the objectives of the school. The professional also intreprets his field to his colleagues and to the community in order that others may understand the program and its accomplishments. In turn, he develops interest in community projects and assists others in pursuing them. Professionals in all fields serve the community in many leadership roles.

THE FUTURE OF THE PROFESSION

Since World War II, physical education in the United States has enjoyed greater status than at any other time in its history. Because of the poor physical condition of many Selective Service inductees and later because of the inferiority of American children to their European counterparts in physical fitness, the nation became aware of a growing problem. President Eisenhower formed a President's Council of Fitness to bring to the attention of all the problem of an unfit citizenry. Throughout the nation, the press gave more favorable coverage than ever before to the activities of those involved in bringing the physical fitness message to the people.

Recent evidence points to a beneficial effect of physical fitness on longevity and especially cardiovascular health. The shortening of the work week and a continuation of a trend toward complete mechanization suggest the need for good physical education in the future. And finally, the need for some new forms of physical activity for those who will spend long periods of time in space adds another dimension to the program in the future. A field of endeavor that has survived several thousand years will continue to flourish in spite of the competition for the school time and the tax dollar.

CONCLUSIONS

People do not become professionals overnight. Most of the burden to instill a professional attitude remains with the teacher education institution and the major department. If students are taught by professors who do not keep up to date, who lack a professional attitude, who do not conduct research or write, and who themselves are not members of professional associations, there is little chance that the student will develop a professional attitude. If the student has no contact with professional growth opportunities during his undergraduate days, there is little likelihood that he will seek them out later. The major department has an obligation that goes far beyond the offerings of courses which satisfy the state's minimum certification requirements.

STUDENT PROJECTS

1. List the ten characteristics you most admire in teachers you have had at all levels of instruction.
2. Review graduate school bulletins to compare academic requirements for admission.
3. Present summaries of the leading professional organizations, especially those open to students.

GLOSSARY OF TERMS

Profession An occupation requiring specialized knowledge, guided by principles, and involving long and intensive academic preparation.

Workshop A seminar emphasizing free discussion and participation by all members.

Institute A short series of meetings on a specific subject.

Clinic A series of meetings on a specific physical activity for the purpose of updating the practitioners.

SELECTED REFERENCES

1. Angell, George. "Physical Education and the New Breed," *Journal of Health, Physical Education and Recreation,* **40** (June 1969), pp. 25-28.
2. Bucher, Charles A. *Foundations of Physical Education,* 5th ed. St. Louis: C. V. Mosby, 1968.
3. Holbrook, Leona. "Education is Our Business." *Journal of Health, Physical Education and Recreation,* **37** (April 1966), pp. 19, 81.
4. Nixon, John E., and Ann E. Jewett. *An Introduction to Physical Education,* 7th ed. Philadelphia: W. B. Saunders, 1969.
5. Ohio Commission on Teacher Education and Professional Standards, *TEPS and the Teaching Profession: A Position Statement and Concerns.* Memorandum to local Teachers Associations. Columbus, Ohio, May 22, 1969.
6. Resick, Matthew C. "Graduate Patterns." Speech presented at the Graduate Education Conference, Washington, January 8, 1967.
7. —————. "Let's Turn Pro," *The Physical Educator,* **17** (December 1960), pp. 135-36.
8. Scott, M. Gladys (ed.). *Research Methods,* 2nd ed. Washington: American Association for Health, Physical Education and Recreation, 1959.

ABCDEFGH798765432